Rachel's Children

Surviving the Second World War

Jean Rodenbough

ALL THINGS
THAT MATTER
PRESS

For Louise –
... Let there be
peace ...
Jean
3-3-11

ISBN: 978-0-9846216-6-8

Library of Congress Control Number: 2010913495

Cover photo: Children's Memorial at Lidice, Poland

Cover design by All Things That Matter Press

Published in 2010 by All Things That Matter Press

*These pages are dedicated to the children of all wars. May there come a time
when no child will ever again experience the consequence of war.*

I wonder if God is despondent,
on the edge of abandonment
with war where terror and hate give impetus
to death over and over
where babies are left to die
for want of will and compassion
where those young enough
to glimpse the future
watch gun and fire become
the common medium of anger.

-Ellen Porter
from "God of Darkness, God of Light"
Some Small Flower of Honesty
Erie, PA:Benetvision. 2009

Our family in Honolulu: My mother, Juliette, brother Bob, me, my father, Col. Philip P. Green

Me, with my two brothers, Robert and Philip Green, Jr.
Hot Springs, Arkansas, in the late 1930's

Foreword

"Who are those men?" I asked my father, pointing to the magazine he was reading. Peering over his shoulder, I could see pictures of several uniformed figures on facing pages, looking off in the distance.

"They're men in the war," he answered.

"Oh. Are these all the people who are in a war?" "No," he responded sadly. "There are many in a war." The time was 1939, and I was looking at an article about events that might widen an international conflict of military actions then taking place in Europe.

I was nearly six and encountering my first awareness of war, although I wasn't quite sure what it meant. My father, an Army pathologist in the Medical Corps, had been a young battle surgeon in the First World War and was severely wounded by shrapnel as he worked in a field hospital in Chateau Thierry, France. Because of the loss of some finger joints in that injury, he no longer could be a surgeon, and eventually changed his field to pathology, but remained in the Army. A year after I asked him about the pictures in the magazine, we left Hot Springs, Arkansas and headed across the Pacific Ocean to Honolulu, where he was to serve a second tour of duty at Tripler Army Hospital. It was there, on December 7, 1941, that I came to know more about war. The Japanese attack on Pearl Harbor that Sunday morning deeply affected us as a family, and my father as a physician, caring for the wounded.

This book is a result of my realization of the effects on me, a child in that time. Such an event left indelible impressions on my psyche, even though my experiences were indirect. In recent years I came to realize how limited my awareness was of how warfare affected many children in that war, and I began searching for personal accounts of those whose experiences were more involved. As indicated in the list of sources at the end of this book, I found numerous stories attesting to the hardships and changes in the lives of children around the world. I have referred to these collections, along with the personal experiences of my friends and new acquaintances. My brief poems are included as commentaries to these stories. In my awareness of the suffering and disasters brought about by war, my concluding pages contain reflections and my conviction that war must become a matter of history only, no longer bringing violence and desecration in its destructive wake.

I wish to thank all those whose stories appear in these pages. I have documented sources not credited within the narrative itself, even when I don't quote directly from an account. The telling of that time, painful and unforgettable, contribute to the growing belief that war inflicts indelible injuries on children that remain for a lifetime. In ways that are always welcome, however, the wisdom acquired through suffering can benefit those who come after us if we are willing to relate one to another without violence, without warfare, without calling on the self-serving evils that exist among nations and individuals. We who have lived during such times of terror and death have the power to speak the words of true peace that overcome sorrow.

INTRODUCTION

A voice is heard in Ramah, lamentation and bitter weeping. Rachel is weeping for her children; she refuses to be comforted for her children, because they are no more. (Jeremiah 31:15)

Rachel, the Good Mother, is searching for her children. They are scattered in shelters, in dark rooms and cellars, in tombs deep in the earth. Their tears wash the air and heal the cries; they listen for what they do not know. But Mother Rachel knows. She weeps in Ramah, and Ramah is everywhere and in every time. She wanders through the barren fields and empty houses, in the darkness of war again. This time it is the World War that follows a World War, identified by various names: The Second World War, the War Against Japanese Aggression, the Great Patriotic War, set within the context of the reach for Lebensraum, and a military defined as the Defense Forces. Again, her children are in the great diaspora, in foreign lands, exiled from their expectations, longing for a return to time that was and seeking what they had yet to know. Her children are innocent. Her children are lost.

To read about these experiences, we must enter another time, and discover our own stories even though they may not be remotely similar to these. In fact, we may need to take time for silence, and even go so far as to remove our sandals symbolically as we step into sacred space. There is trauma to be discovered here: That of warfare. These stories are about childhood spent during World War II. Some of those who speak were affected directly by this time, others experienced less immediate and direct effects.

Wars once were fought among warriors. Today, the statistics reveal that somewhere between 95% and 98% of those killed and injured are non-combatants: Children, women, and the elderly.[1] Wars have become impersonal, and in that very act have become ever more personal, as it is the individuals who suffer, who cope, who struggle to survive, who die. The author of one collection of accounts about the war and how children

---

[1] Joan Chittister, OSB, speech July 2008.

were affected writes, "World War II would become the first modern war in which more civilians than soldiers were killed or maimed … we [children] had survived a global conflict in which more children had been killed and maimed than in all previous wars in the world."[2]

How best to describe what happens to children? One way, of course, is by sharing their personal stories. At times, however, words alone will not reach the depths of truth embedded deeply in the psyche of those who were affected not only physically, but also within their inner spirits. Poetry is an additional way to continue the conversation between the historical, biographical story and the one that lies beneath history as a timeless testimony. There is truth in poetry which promotes reflection on what is first read as story and reminiscence. The accounts here seek resolution of the pain described, in part through the poems as commentary, in an attempt to discover the inner narrative of the soul. Rachel, Good Mother, Grieving Mother, may find her children and bring them back to herself in these words that are only symbols for something indescribable and unspoken.

The Children

Rachel wanders the earth, seeking
her lost ones, the children of war,
for new Herods have been here
stealing the lives and bodies
of the young.

They lie in hospitals, graves, the streets,
caught in the web of gunfire and bombs.
Their games and outings interrupted,
they have left the classroom and their books;
the lessons are over.

---

[2] Emmy E. Werner, *Through the Eyes of Innocents: Children Witness World War II*, 1.

Rachel's Children

Ramah is anywhere;
we are all Rachel now, searching,
weeping.

THE BEGINNING

*Fear cannot bear truth without trust. It takes
one who holds our vulnerable lives in strength
to convince. And even then ...even then,
we hear the distant rumble, the gathering storm.
"War is very bad," we are told. We feel it in our bones,
those genes from a dark past remind us.*

The year 1939 marked the beginning of a war that would eventually affect the entire world in one way or another for the next six years. Although the United States would not enter until 1941, in England and continental Europe, life began to change dramatically following the German military's march into Poland September 1, 1939. Hitler's armies showed little mercy for the inhabitants of countries considered necessary for German expansion, its *Lebensraum*.

Children began to hear their elders speak of impending war and then its beginning, without a full understanding of such consequences. Parents tried to reassure their children by saying war was not good, but that little ones would be all right. Two days after Germany invaded Poland, Great Britain and France declared war on Germany, and Warsaw fell to the German army by the end of September. In the beginning, France was spared from invasion, and children believed assurances that they would be safe. Fathers in France and elsewhere, however, soon began to be drafted into the armed services.

*A duck flies out of the pond. A rooster crows.
The field begins to wear brown. Grasshoppers
lose their summer green; the music fades
from their wings. Cannon boom like drums
of war over the hill, as dark-clad troops follow
the commands of death. A baby shrieks,
a summons comes to a home in France.
Poland is lost.*

In Great Britain, preparations began for war, mainly for purposes of defense at first. Civilians received gas masks, instructions on the use of air raid shelters were dispersed, blackouts were initiated. The children made up games about these measures, and practiced wearing gas masks during school time. Pre-schoolers were given masks with Mickey Mouse faces, which delighted them. For the young, this playful attitude helped obscure the anxiety they sensed in their elders.

As in some cartoon movie
they strut around wearing
Mickey Mouse faces, giggling
at one another until mothers
call out "Don't laugh at war!"
and bewildered, the children are silent.
Slowly, like some wounded beast
calling to her mate, the sirens
start up, wail and shriek, for what
may or may not be a moment of death.
In the thick darkness
no one can see the fear on children's
faces, no one can hear over the loud
siren song their question, "Is it real?"

War became real to the children in Scotland when a major incident occurred involving the British Navy and a German air raid on the Orkney Islands. The British ship, *Royal Oak,* was blown up in Scapa Flow, and some 800 lives were lost, including boys in military training. The *Luftwaffe* became more active in the weeks to follow, and Scottish children observed the German symbols painted on the planes. A U-boat torpedoed a British ship and then rescued the British crew, as if to display some small act of humanity toward their victims.[3]

Yet elsewhere the Germans were not so compassionate. The killing of a pet dog in Poland is symbolic of another aspect of the violent military

------

[3] Bessie Shea, *Through the Eyes of Innocents,* 13.

character.[4] This kind of behavior, unfortunately, does not show favoritism, and whenever human beings are engaged in hostilities, baser behavior is commonplace. Mercy can be a fickle partner.

> *The family dog guards with canine intensity;*
> *protective, warning, then jerks upward at the deadly shot.*
> *He is no longer a sentry or harbinger or defender.*
> *There are some who dislike dogs. This one lies silent at last.*
> *Mercy, even so, is never completely gone.*
> *It passes through, blessing and weeping.*

Long before the war in Europe became reality, war in Asia had been waged for a decade, beginning in the 1930's with Japan's invasion of China. There too, children were the innocents deeply affected by what was taking place in their country. There were calls for resistance that were announced even in the classrooms full of those too young as yet to take up arms.[5]

> *It is good sometimes to interrupt classes.*
> *Not this time. Words that turn innocence*
> *into fear. Words that urge resistance. Words*
> *to teach the power of hate. Words not spoken*
> *yet present to shape minds of schoolchildren*
> *and strengthen resolve. Not all who heard*
> *the words spoken and words behind the speech*
> *would graduate, except to another life. This*
> *is the new school for beginners in grief.*

After the conflicts began in China and in Europe, other nations were drawn into the web of war. The United States met its own destiny with war on December 7, 1941, with the Japanese air attack on Pearl Harbor, the naval base on the Hawaiian island of Oahu. Children in Honolulu

---

[4] Janine Phillips, *Through the Eyes of Innocents,* 13.
[5] Andrew Tu, *No Long Silent: World-Wide Memories of the Children of World War II,* 21.

and children on the "mainland" were initiated into the experience of fear, anxiety, uncertainty, and sorrow before they had reached the maturity to understand such events. American children knew that their country had entered what would be called World War II. My own life was forever changed. My family lived in Honolulu at the time, where my father was a doctor in an Army hospital. Across the Pacific Ocean, Japanese children were also learning of this attack on the United States, and reacted to the news with their own fears and anxieties. Mixed with these childhood emotions was also that which would bring about its own poisoning effects: Patriotism colored by a need to achieve victory over the enemies. The enemy would become the evil one intent on destroying one's own people, from the child's perspective.

> *My father heard the news;*
> *my brothers heard the news;*
> *my mother heard and wept.*
> *We all knew the news brought*
> *change to our lives forever.*
>
> *The woman who ironed for us*
> *wept, because her sons were*
> *in two armies, two armies*
> *who would be killing*
> *each other. As in our*
> *Civil War, where brother*
> *fought brother, she could*
> *tell us what war is like*
> *for mothers, for fathers.*
> *We learned only half*
> *the equation but that*
> *was enough for us.*

Children in Hawaii, in particular those on the island of Oahu, were the most directly affected of all the American territories and the mainland United States. Their proximity meant that the first day of battle was waged on their home turf within their hearing and sight. Although children across the embattled nations elsewhere knew of war first hand most fully, for these sheltered ones in what seemed to be secure locations, war began in a horrifying manner, in their perceptions. The traumatic effect of deafening sounds of planes and booms from defensive fire were psychologically muted for some time.[6] It would never be erased from their memories. As one of the children remembered that day:

Most of us lived in the central and eastern parts of Honolulu ... and probably had arisen by 8:00 a.m. or shortly thereafter. When we looked or went outside, we were greeted by billowing black smoke from the early Pearl Harbor strike and some of the planes circling back for additional runs against the backdrop of small puffs from our anti-aircraft guns .... Many families eventually tuned in [to the radio] and heard Webley Edwards broadcasting news of the war. We also heard many rumors during and following the attack, including reports of saboteurs poisoning our water supplies and parachutists landing on the mountaintops. The Pearl Harbor attack, of course, had an immediate impact on all our lives, for some real fear and for others a sense of bewilderment. Few of us were in the combat zones, but some of us had fathers or other family members who did experience the chaos of Pearl Harbor and vicinity.[7]

Only one day out of a life
brings on the cataclysmic
effects of a lifetime
not yet spent.

Black smoke on a Sunday morning,
planes appear from the sea
to interrupt the December weekend.
Sirens scream through streets
indiscriminate of homes and buildings

---

[6] Paul Wysard, *Children of the Storm*, 23.

[7] John Bowles, author and editor, *The Day Our World Changed: December 7, 1941: Punahou '52 Remembers Pearl Harbor*, 15-16.

where Japanese, Chinese, Hawaiian
and wahinie neighbored. Church bells
call worshipers to services while whine
of bullets and flash of light accent
the morning bright with hope transformed
into fearful surprise.

Thus children in American territories joined their counterparts around the world, by spending the next few years in a climate of war and its accompanying horrors. It was not a time of glory, no matter how many patriotic speeches would be delivered, no matter how many inspiring songs were sung and encouraging prayers offered. It was instead, a time of war.

nothing to celebrate
no bands no drums
for marching
only surreal sounds
that buzz and whine
about our ears and the boom
of war that shrill quality in the air

My own experience as an eight-year-old in Honolulu was shared with classmates many times after my mother, brother and I returned to the "mainland." My father remained in Hawaii where he was a pathologist with the Army Medical Corps. After the attack, he was to continue his service as Commanding Officer of the North Sector Tripler General Hospital. He remained at that post until the end of the war, when he was assigned to the Army hospital at Ft. Hamilton in Brooklyn, NY. By then I was in grade 7B[3] at Public School 104, and wrote this essay for a class assignment, dated February 21, 1946. (This is an unabridged version.)

A Day I Shall Remember

It started just like most Sunday mornings usually begin in our household. Everyone was asleep but me.

We were living in Honolulu, as Daddy is in the Army, and had been ordered there. In fact, we had been living in Honolulu since August of 1940.

But to return to the story, I was the only one awake, as I said before. I heard the dull booming of guns, but paid no attention to them, as the army and navy practice firing frequently.

Finally Mother and Daddy woke up, (my brother was still sleeping soundly) and as Daddy always listens to the news, he turned on the radio for the 9:00 broadcast. The first message that came to our ears was: "This is the real McCoy! Pearl Harbor is under attack! The Japanese have made a sneak attack on the Island of Oahu!" We were naturally taken aghast. Daddy announced that he was going to eat breakfast and go straight down to the hospital. I didn't feel like eating very much breakfast myself, I was so frightened.

We went out on our small back porch and gazed up at the sky. There were puffs of black smoke here and there which showed that the anti-aircraft guns were busy too. Fortunately, we were in little danger ourselves, because we were approximately 15 miles from Pearl Harbor.

It was a rather strange and frightening day, and one to be remembered, too.

An account of December 7 is shown here, from notes my brother, Robert B. Green, age 16 at the time, made as events transpired, with abbreviations and punctuation as in the original copy. There is some editing for clarity.

Sunday, December 7, 1941:

7:45 – Heavy firing continued to 9:15

9:00 – Turned on radio and heard that Oahu had been attacked – all Army men ordered to posts.

Telephone lines jammed but soon Dad was phoned to report to Tripler [an Army Hospital]. Basic announcements by very excited announcers mixed with rotten canned music. "Don't use phone; all civilians please remain off the streets," etc. [radio announcements]

10:15 – First real news announcement: Sporadic air attack on Oahu. Rising sun sighted on wings of airplanes.

10:16 – Gov. Poindexter declares state of emergency exists in the

Territory. Many organizations call truck drivers, chauffeurs, motor boat operators, etc. to report to Kewalo Basin. (Sweep Jap mines) "All T.H. Davies and American Factors truck and motorcycle drivers report to National Guard Armory at once."

10:20 – doctors (mostly Jap names) ordered to report to Tripler.

10:25 – "Trucks will leave Pier 5 at 11:00 and go over certain streets; all Naval ammunition depot workers be on those streets to be taken to work."

10:30 – Urgent call for more doctors (many names) to report to Tripler at once to care for large number of wounded.

10:34 – call for ALL available truck and motorcycles and drivers.

10:45 – employees of Oahu Prison, Territory Hospital, Kawaialoa Training School, Waimanu Home called to work. Male civilian employees report to Pearl Harbor.

10:55 – Disaster Committee chairmen report to 24-hour duty. Blackout to be announced later.

11:07 – All male P[earl] H[arbor] workers report to Oahu Railway Station.

11:10 – Am[erican] Leg[ion] members report to clubhouse. Young Bros. employees report to boathouse.

11:12 – Inter-Island sailings and flyings canceled.

11:21 – Washington announces attack. Second attack.

11:30 – U[niversity of] H[awaii] Senior R.O.T.C. ordered to report at once.

11:37 – Orders in foreign languages (many earlier orders were repeated in various languages all morning).

11:40 – Army orders radio [stations] off the air.

12:00 – Heavy firing.

1:30 – Dad called to see if we were safe.

Hear many false rumors during the day about parachutists, condition of air fields, P.H., deaths, casualties, etc.

A boat on which Dad had planned to go fishing (but didn't) was machine-gunned and a Captain got some skin shot off his back.

3:30 – Provisional Police called out.

4:15 – Federal Martial Law in effect.

4:30 – Boil all water.

4:40 – All employees of construction companies report to Kewalo Basin. Signal Corps civil employees report to [Ft.] Shafter. Unemployed report for jobs with U.S.E.D.

5:35 – Gov. Poindexter announces Martial Law, complete blackout, etc.

6:00 – Dad calls, won't be home.

6:20 – Poindexter says there are 187 civilian casualties. No dealer can raise food prices, sell to other than regular customers, or sell more than usual amounts.

9:15 – Many flashes and explosions towards town, tracer bullets, A.A. shells, one burning plane. (It was our men at Fort Shafter shooting down a U.S. MARINE plane. The pilot bailed out safely, and was just about the maddest man on the island.)

My Father Kept a Log

This account was written by my father, Lt. Col. Philip P. Green (later a full Colonel), detailing his experience December 7. This was typed by him without paragraph breaks, and blunt language is used. He was a pathologist, stationed at Tripler Army Hospital at the time. It is presented here as he typed it, with some minor editing. He began his military service right out of medical school during World War I, and was seriously wounded in France by shrapnel as he worked at a field hospital. He decided to remain in the Army after healing from his wounds.

Sunday, Dec. 7

7:55 – Heavy gunfire continuously. Wondered at Navy doing so much target practice. At about 8:30 got up and prepared for shower. Turned on radio and caught last of a sentence "...all civilians stay off the streets," followed by canned music. Realized this was the real thing. Repeated radio announcements of attack and warning to stay off streets. Dressed and ate hurried breakfast, heard order on radio for all men to report to posts. Telephone from hospital to come at once. All quiet on streets. Cars with soldiers and sailors racing ewa *(sic)*. Going by Prospect Street around edge of Punchbowl. Saw one moderate black smoke Makai side of Pearl Harbor, another very large very dense cloud on Mauka side. Guessed it must be one of the Doheny oil tanks. No gunfire or bombs at the moment. Reached hospital. Ambulances arriving and patients being unloaded. Litters covered with blood, no time to wipe off, load on another. Corridors filled with patients on litters. New wards turned over to us two days before, no equipment. Trucks unloading beds and mattresses. Patients being laid on beds at front of ward while other beds being set up and dressed at other end. Ran to receiving office, grabbed a bunch of dressings and adhesive out of a packing box, carried it to ward. Found a basin and filled it, pulled cotton from roll and started dressings. Most of patients in coveralls covered with dirt, large wounds, part of them still undressed, many still bleeding, some had to be tourniquetted. Found some iodine. Civilian doctors arriving. Operating teams set up in operating room and worst cases started thru. Worked on wards wherever there seemed most need. Other laboratory officers doing same thing. As civilians got dressings in hand, went to laboratory. Found three sergeants all out helping where they could. Pvt. Devine had taken charge, started rapid production of intravenous saline. Told him to add dextrose. Found blood typing for transfusions being handled efficiently by hematology force. Helped here and there in wards, in operating room giving transfusions. Checked on morgue. Found all dead from Hickam [Field] being evacuated here instead of to mortuary. Finally got orders issued to have tags. Set up an identification squad to search for papers and to fingerprint the rest. Put overflow into new recreation building after throwing out benches. Capt. Crawford detailed to organize a squad to secure personal possessions from clothing. Horrible sights everywhere. Never saw such an infuriated group of men and nurses and civilian women helpers. Realized that when this got to the mainland there would be the same fury there and none of the rather sorrowful resolve on 1917 but instead a merciless war of extermination against the brown SOBs. Finally night. Windows draped with blankets. Laboratory worked all night with saline and blood typing. Got a little sleep on the floor in office. Much fireworks about 10 PM followed by glow in sky beyond Red Hill lasting about 30 minutes. Watched till fragments started falling around. Went inside. At graying of dawn small group of very fast planes flew [from] Makai very low over hospital. About 10 seconds later terrific gunfire, machine guns and heavy stuff. Sudden loud rather sharp explosion very near, sounded just over hospital. Decided better get on shoes and go downstairs. Found not a bomb but probably an AA shell. Fragments punctured two cars in front of building, tagged two civilians behind building near heating plant and soldier on porch of guard house across street. None serious. Later learned planes were our own and nervous gunner had set off the uproar. Washed face and went down for breakfast. Things quieter Monday. Great deal of work all over place. Got most of morgue and recreation hall guests cleared out Monday afternoon. Never will be able to get that hall out of my mind. Never saw such a wholesale mess even in France. Got a bit unpleasant by Monday night. Someone got oil of lavender and sprinkled around. Never want to smell lavender again. Got home a few minutes Tuesday. Found four refugee families in the house. All behaving well but one fool who was chattering her head off and complaining of everything. Bob warned me on the porch. Mother had gone to commissary for food. Jumped on by the fool as I went in. Wanted dressings, iodine, a cot for her brat "who can't sleep on the cushions on the floor," etc. Gave her hell and told her to shut up and behave like an adult. Approving nods from other women. Mother came in. Behaving well and showing plenty of control and courage. Went back to hospital. Next few days gradually quieting down, lots of running around fitting up laboratories at other places, drawing blood for bank, listening to extraordinary rumors. Read in paper a disgusting cheerup-we-are-with-you announcement from Eleanor [Roosevelt]. Several comments from women similarly disgusted. Finally got to spend night at home on 19th.

Excerpt from a letter dated Sunday afternoon, December 7, 1941, written by my brother Philip P. Green, Jr., a student at Princeton University, to our mother shows his reaction to the news of the attack on Pearl Harbor during the time he is writing the letter.

.... I'm afraid I messed up another mil[itary] sci[ience] test yesterday. Instead of a map, they gave us an aerial photo on which hills, etc., behind which to place the batteries, were practically indistinguishable so far as I was concerned. And a large part of the problem was something which we hadn't had in class, but stuff which all the seniors learned at camp last summer.

[*Here, the handwriting becomes larger and reflects excitement and haste in the writing*]:

The news flash just came over the air about the attack on Hawaii. There's nothing I can say now. Hope you are alright and that none of you will be harmed. The flashes are coming in over all the stations, and there is naturally great excitement all over campus.

Sunday night:

News continues to flow in. The undergraduates here have had quite a reaction to it. Some of them are holding wild drinking parties. Most feel that they will be called into one of the services soon. The excitement is immense – almost hysteria.

I can't imagine what caused the Japs to take such a step. They must have been driven to a state of desperation by that blockade.

Some of the fellows here have been sending cables to their folks and relatives in Hawaii, but I feel that the lines will be crowded enough anyway and that you will let me know if there's anything wrong.

I wish I could have been there to see it all and all of your reactions. I hope you didn't get hysterical or worry to the point of getting sick. With Bob there, there shouldn't have been any trouble that could be avoided. I guess Dad had to go down to the hospital.

The activity in the States is terrific. All reserve officers in this district are being called to duty, I think, and they're starting listening center details to work, etc. Mayor LaGuardia is issuing his usual excited communiqués. He warned all Japanese in this part of the country to stay in their homes until they could be investigated.

I hope Hawaii won't be molested anymore. I don't think they could gain anything more now that we're on the alert.

The question everyone is asking is, "How, with all Hawaii's vaunted defenses, did the Japs manage to get close enough to launch their aerial attack? Everyone seems to feel that there was an awful boner somewhere.

I wonder how soon, or whether, they'll evacuate you all. No doubt it would be too dangerous at the moment.

Well, nothing can be served by my speculation. This letter will probably be much delayed anyway.

Much love to all,

Bill

On the 40ᵗʰ anniversary of the attack on Pearl Harbor, 1981, I wrote a piece for the local Greensboro, NC paper, the News & Record.

Christmas, 1941, Hawaii

Christmas for our family was different that year: Different because we were far away from our southern roots, different because war had disrupted our lives. The time was 1941, the place was Honolulu, Hawaii. My father was a doctor in the Army, stationed at Tripler General Hospital. The morning of December 7 had burst open in terror. The dull thuds of distant guns and bombs out in the harbor imposed a frightening and irregular rhythm on the day. Snatches of events, brief pictures of the day, come back to me even now, 40 years later: The intermittent radio announcements that kept us in touch with this new experience of war; the calls for Japanese-speaking doctors; the nervous pleas by Webley Edwards and other announcers to remain calm; instructions on civilian security; precautions for purifying our water supply.

There was the anxiety of seeing my father leave, not to be heard from for several days, the efforts of my mother and brother to retain normalcy in the midst of panic, the calls from friends at Schofield Barracks in need of housing. We were able to accommodate more than a dozen women and children in our home that was well away from any areas of danger.

For an eight-year-old, war brought a mixture of experience and reactions. There was both fear and excitement, a brilliance of moments outlined in dark dangers. We third-graders learned how to scramble into deep trenches at the sound of an air-raid siren, hoping we were merely going through a practice drill, wishing that there had been enough gas masks available for small faces.

At home, the growing collection of children played thoughtless tricks on the older, worried ones. We pulled an old and harmless artillery shell once used as a gate marker out from under the house and called everyone to come see the "bomb" that had landed in the yard. Our black-out shades were decorated with chalk drawings of hibiscus blossoms by one of the Navy wives staying with us. We learned to turn on lights only in the living room where we had the black shades; we grew accustomed to the khaki, angle-necked flashlights with the red paint over the glass. War did have its novelties for a child never trained to know its horror.

That Christmas we had no tree to decorate. The entire shipment had been sunk on the way over from California. Instead, my brother, always resourceful, drilled holes in a broomstick, running straightened coat hangers through them, and wrapping the wires in green crepe paper. By the time we had our traditional decorations and tinsel hanging from the "boughs," we were convinced that this was the best tree ever.

Gradually, our emergency guests were finding roomier lodging, and we became a single family again. We grew accustomed to changes. Friends would call to say good-bye, having been notified to leave in a matter of hours on the next military ship back to the "Mainland." Some, I recall, had to leave Christmas turkeys still in the oven for their men to take care of along with the shipping of furniture and other household belongings later as time and space would allow.

We wondered when our name would come up to leave. As it turned out, we were overlooked for a few months when my father was transferred to another hospital unit, and we did not leave until March, zigzagging our way through seas and seasickness to San Francisco.

War from a child's perspective needs time to draw the lines clearly. The moments of fun were few. More often, what is remembered now are the cold, tight feelings in the pit of the stomach, the chilling sound of sirens and silence that followed, broken by cries of Minah birds, brief and sudden farewells to playmates, anxious waiting for news of those in battle, the never-knowing- where-we'll-be-tomorrow uncertainties. An eight-year-old knows instinctively, as well as anyone, that war is the worst of existence. The knowledge comes as briefly and clearly as the flash of anti-aircraft fire against a December Hawaiian sky. The effects linger a lifetime: The early fears that mistake lightning bugs in North Carolina the next summer for Nazi spies hiding behind the shrubbery; that interpret National Guard maneuvers as another invasion; the later fears that one's own children will experience war first-hand.

Remembrance of war is a heavy thought in December, in the time that we celebrate the coming of the Prince of Peace. Do we note the irony of a nation's concern over the growing strength of peace movements throughout the world and the fear they present more danger than uncontrolled arms build-ups? There are better ways to spend one's early years than in war. There is the alternative of spending one's aging years in a time of peace among nations. We who survived that war-time Christmas in 1941 can hope that we need not fear the call to lay down our arms in order to embrace our enemies. Yet it is an impossible hope – a scandal – and the thread we cling to as we go over the edge.

The following excerpts from her diary are from Jane Wylie's account of the attack on Pearl Harbor and the days and months following. Living in Honolulu, she describes her experiences through the eyes of a 10-year-old. Some editing has been made for clarity.[8]

Dear Diary

Sunday, December 7, 1941 6:45
I woke up this morning and Mr. White said he saw nine Jap planes fly overhead in perfect formation. I turned on the radio; it said that Oahu was being attacked by unidentified planes. Later it was announced that they were Japanese planes. The radio was turned off the rest of the day. I went up to my girl friend's house but she was at Sunday School so I told her mother. She went in and turned on her radio.

I went and sat on the porch with my mother, who was writing a letter. All at once we saw a big fire somewhere near McCully. I went up the hill across the street where I could see better. It was probably a bomb.

During an air-raid you are not supposed to go out in the street, or use your telephone. My father went down and got my girl friend from Sunday School. A bomb also landed in Lewers and Cook.

P.S. Today was Helen Bowles' birthday. We ate ice cream and cake in the blackout.

---

[8] With appreciation to John Bowles for sharing this account.

January 3
Today some soldiers made a camp across the street from the Bowles. We watched them put up their tents and cut grass. After a while they cut down trees to camouflage the tents and trucks.

January 11
Today we went down to get fingerprinted. They give you a little card to carry with you. It has fingerprints in it, in case you are hit by shrapnel. I carry mine around my neck.

January 21
Today we got our gas masks at the first aid station. They give you a little booklet on first aid, blackout, gas masks, etc. The gas mask is made of rubber and has glass goggles to see through. There is a can at the bottom, and it has charcoal and chemicals to purify the air.

March 14
Today there was an air-raid alarm. I was at my music lessons; my teacher was writing what I was to do. Then all at once we heard the alarm. My mother happened to be passing by. She drove up and stopped. We (Helen and I) were just starting for a friend's house when we saw my mother. We had ten minutes to get home. A cop stopped us and told us to stop, but we went around the corner, and continued our trip home.

April 5
Today I watched the Aquitania go out. I think my friend's cousins went on it. On April 4 they told them to be on board between 4:00 and 6:00. Then the next day it went out. It has four smoke stacks.
Today was Easter. Even though eggs are expensive we had dyed eggs.

April 27
Today Mauna Loa erupted. They do not announce it over the radio because it would not be so good on the blackout. Mr. Davis was talking to someone in Hilo on the telephone. He asked him how the fire-works

were, and the censor cut him off.

May 11
Today Washington released the news about the bombing of Tokyo. They said it was done by Army planes. Mt. Asama is erupting also (in Japan).

June 2
There are three more days until vacation. Today our air-raid shelters were finished. Beatrice Chang and I dusted off the benches. They have been working on them about a month.

The following is an excerpt from an address by Helen Bowles Nicholson at an assembly in Philadelphia, 1991, at Germantown Friends School. The writer is the sister of John Bowles, editor of The Day Our World Changed: December 7, 1941: Punahou '52 Remembers Pearl Harbor. *She describes here the experience of her grandparents, former Quaker missionaries to Japan.*

Another Perspective

All of this [her story of the December 7 attack] is the easy part to relate. The difficulty comes when I try to share the distress of my grandparents, who had spent 40 years of their lives working at Tokyo Friends School and with the peace movement in Japan. My grandfather's life had been threatened when he went to Korea in the 1930's to protest the behavior of the Japanese occupying that country. My grandparents were forced to leave Tokyo in September of 1941, when their Japanese friends informed them that their own lives were endangered by association with my grandparents. My father wired them the passage fare, and they were permitted to sail from Yokohama with only their Bible and the clothes on their backs.

Grandfather set out on December 8, 1941, to call on various Japanese-American families on Oahu. He spent his energy and every working moment in the years to come helping those whose loved ones had been sent to internment camps on the Mainland and whose homes and businesses and temples were subject to U.S. Government takeover. He managed to keep his pacifism and conveyed to us, his grandchildren, his Quaker faith in the basic goodness of *most* people. In retrospect, I realize what a deep sense of personal failure and disillusionment he must have felt. He and grandmother returned to Japan in 1947 for a reunion with their Japanese friends, and they retained their close ties until their deaths.

My second grade classmate at Lincoln School, Helen Haxton Bode, of Kailua, Hawaii, wrote of her memories of the day of the Japanese attack and the following years. (Ironically, I had planned to spend the night with Helen Saturday December 6, but my mother was not feeling well and my father asked me to plan for this another time.) Her account follows, with some minor editing.

I Remember

I could see the "Zeroes" flying all around Pearl Harbor and thereabouts from my bedroom in Makiki, and remember hearing Webley Edwards continuously saying, "This is not maneuvers – this is the real McCoy." We (family) went to my uncle's house on top of Mott Smith Drive, above Roosevelt High School. He had a very high-powered telescope, so we could see the fire and smoke, etc. at Pearl Harbor.

We had a blackout imposed on us and the house had to be completely dark – not a peephole of light could be seen from outside. My Dad was a "warden" who would patrol the neighborhood for light leaks. Every neighborhood had a volunteer warden.

A bomb shelter was dug in the back yard and stocked with food and supplies. I hated it, as there were often centipedes in there! We children were the last ones issued a gas mask. (They had to add extra rubber to fit the smaller faces of kids.) I remember it took a long time for us to get one. Then when we did get one, we had to lug it everywhere! We claimed to each other: "It is a load off our minds, but a load on our shoulders." We were all asked to wear ID bracelets.

Later on, our Punahou campus was taken over by the Army Corps of Engineers and Army forces. We eventually had to relocate to the University of Hawaii's Elementary School.

Correspondence was inspected to and from Hawaii, and our paper currency was stamped HAWAII over the face of the bill.

These are some of the things I remember. I'm sure there are many more I could conjure up *ad nauseum*. One final note: My parents sent my brother Bill and me to Portland, Oregon to live with my aunt and uncle. We got there by Navy transport. We had to zigzag all the way across the ocean to avoid enemy torpedoes. We had a large convoy of ships with us, all zigzagging. I spent my 4th and half of 5th grades in Oregon; then my parents sent for us to come back. The war was still on, so we had a lot of red tape to go through to return, and came back the same way, Navy transport. I remember the ships were very hot and crowded, and the sleeping area was like a large dormitory with adults and children all mixed up. (Very tedious trips!)

Punahou schooling was still at the University for the other half of 5th grade and all of 6th. We got our campus back for the 7th grade, and by then the war was over.

Needless to say, I had a great time in Oregon. That year they had a "silver thaw." It was such a treat for a kid from Hawaii to play in the snow!

My high school classmate, Patricia Halvorsen Holladay, recalls learning about the attack on Pearl Harbor when she lived in the community of Steilacoom, Washington, near Tacoma.

Here at Home

My girlfriend and I left for church on the hill on a beautiful, sunny morning December 7. Only a light coat was needed. After church, my girlfriend's older brothers came racing up the hill on their bikes yelling, "We're at war! We're at war!" She rode back home with them, leaving me to run many blocks to my home.

I found my father, a doctor who joined the National Guard the previous year, calmly working on a new garden beside a new patio in our new old home. He was planting tulips when I ran up. He acted as if there were all the time in the world to complete his job, and he told me that he would be packing soon and reporting in at Ft. Lewis [the Army post nearby]. He calmed my fears. He returned the day's beauty. And he did indeed pack and leave.

The next spring, the tulips burst through the earth in a pattern that spelled I LUV U.

From Hong Kong

This reflection on Christmas 1941 is written by Jean Woo, who was living in Hong Kong at the time. Her father was an engineer who later directed the construction of the air base in Chonqing where the "Flying Tigers" were stationed. In addition to this account, she sent an e-mail with reflections, as quoted below.

I was sitting on a rather high chair having my hair combed (to go to school) by a servant when I looked out the 4th floor balcony on Nathan Road, Kowloon and saw the Japanese planes dropping bombs on Hong Kong island. The years that followed I experienced lots of bombing, running for our lives with the family, hunger, etc. Therefore for many years I could not relate to the Japanese. In college many times people would mistake me as a Japanese because of my round face. I regarded that as a real insult. Then I made friends with the Japanese Christians in the Asian Christian Women's Conference (ACWC). Now I still have many Japanese friends, love Japanese food, etc. Over Christmas a nephew who just got his Ph.D. from Harvard married a Japanese girl. His parents were furious! Many Chinese cannot forgive what the Japanese in WWII. But I no longer have this grudge.

Below is the account of her first wartime Christmas, December 1941.

Since December 8th we had been under self-imposed house arrest. No one except the young maid Chun Har (Spring Mist) had ventured down the four flights of stairs. She was able to find food, heaven knows how, for members of our household once in a while. Yes, only once in a while because practically all stores were closed and the "wet market" no longer existed. Japanese soldiers marched up and down the streets. We could see them from our balcony. One day a soldier aimed his bayoneted rifle at a pedestrian [who was] crossing the street without bowing 90 degrees to pay respect. Quickly my aunts pulled me in and from then on we stopped going to the balcony, not even to pass the time of our boring days.

A man from my grandmother's village was on the kitchen staff of the near-by Pui Ching School, now used as headquarters for the occupying Japanese army. Cooking for the soldiers was his job. When he measured rice into the huge cooking pot, he would put more rice than necessary, and secretly stuffed the leftover after meals into a container, then smuggled it out and brought it to our house. What he brought was never enough for our family but at least we had some staple food regularly. That was also the first time I tasted Japanese rice, which is a slightly sticky, short grain variety we are now familiar with, used in sushi.

We hardly had any visitors except for this kind man. If we heard footsteps up the stairway, members of the household, all women, would get panicky. Great Grandma was in her 80's, and somewhat confused, so that kind of noise would not alarm her. Grandma was about 60. Even that age seemed ancient to me. I had asked her once, "Grandma, why is the skin on your face all folded up?" So she was not at risk. But the rest of the women, my aunts and their cousins, would put on Chun Har's clothes to pretend they were peasant women. They dipped wet fingers in the charcoal stove and applied ashes on their faces, to hide their youth and beauty. I was spared all of this. No Japanese soldier, if one were to come up the stairs, would look twice at a skinny little girl like me.

Then came Christmas Eve. There would not be any service at the church for sure. No caroling this year either – it would be very unlikely to have groups of cheerful people in white robes singing "Silent Night" on those ghostly, empty streets. Silently, Big Aunt brought in her pot of poinsettias from the balcony, which had survived since the year before. It had a few weak blossoms and some lonesome, malnourished leaves. She found some tinsel and some cotton balls from pill bottles to put on the branches. It did look a bit like Christmas. But I doubted Santa Claus could walk past the barricades and Japanese soldiers without being noticed. So definitely he would not come. Not this year.

Christmas morning I discovered to my great surprise that there was a tiny package under the poinsettias. Wrapped in red tissue paper with a ribbon across it, it had my name on it. Quickly I opened it and found two little cookies. Big Aunt or someone thoughtful had planned ahead, saved and hidden them before all other cookies were consumed, so that I did have a present for Christmas.

It was a memorable Christmas.

The following is an essay recounting another 1941 Christmas, in California, by John Witherspoon. His father was in the Army at the time of the attack on Pearl Harbor.

A Blacked-Out Christmas

Oh! How I wanted to get to sleep. I was too excited. And Kenny kept asking, "Are you awake?" Did you hear that noise? Was it on the roof?"

Kenny. Why did he have to be here? I had heard Mom and Grandma talking about giving some of my presents to him. Needed to make sure that he had something under the tree. His family's sudden arrival from Pearl Harbor after the bombing had spoiled Christmas. The war was bad enough with the adults worrying about everything from what was going to be rationed to which male family member would join which service. Already, Dad was training in the Mohave Desert and Uncle Vance was in Navy flight school. Even Grandpa was talking about re-joining the Navy, after being retired for so many years.

I guess it was really the Japs' fault. Their sneak attack really got everybody upset. None of us neighborhood kids knew exactly where Pearl Harbor was. It seemed somewhat farther away than Oakland, maybe as far as LA, but we got ready for them. Adolph, Jerry, Gopher, Frankie, me and our leader Smurdon soon had the alley behind our house barricaded and facing toward the Bay from where we thought the attack would come.

Then Mr. Garberro had driven in, and ran us off. So we went to the empty lot between our house and Frankie's and dug trenches. Soon we were pulling clods of dirt from the ground and began pelting one another. The threat of invasion was temporarily replaced by the need to insure that no part of each other's clothing or exposed anatomy went un-smeared with mud. I knew that things weren't normal when no adult took particular notice and exception to my mud man appearance when later I returned home.

Then came the adult argument about the placing of the Christmas Tree. Normally, it went in the far left corner of the front room. "But," my grandfather argued, "we'll have to black-out two windows if we put it there."

"We're going to need to black-out all the windows anyway," Grandma retorted.

"Why don't we just black-out Christmas," said Uncle Howard, "and not put the lights on the tree in the first place."

"Black-out Christmas?" I wondered. "How can Christmas be blacked-out?"

Perhaps noticing the disappointment spreading across my face, my mother, glaring at her brother, proclaimed, "We're going to have lights, Howie, just count on it."

Then Grandma said, pointing to the far corner, "And it's going over there."

And that, of course, is where the tree went. Grandma had a way of speaking that announced the end of debate. But it didn't end my worry. The idea of a blacked-out Christmas along with the previous arrival of Kenny and his family was worrisome. Christmas was not turning out to be what I had anticipated.

It didn't help that Kenny was wild. He climbed trees that were forbidden to me and my buddies. He inspected closets that were off limits. He played with my grandpa's tools, got into the paint locker, turned on radios, smoked some of my aunt's cigarettes and climbed out on the roof of the house. All such actions would have brought the wrath of any number of adults down on my head had I been the transgressor. But all Kenny received for the many errors of his ways were slight rebukes and sometimes even praise.

"Now, Kenny, Mrs. Adler doesn't want you messing around in her closet," said his mother.

"Jeez, that kid can climb like a monkey," admired my Aunt Jane as Kenny waved from near the top of the apple tree that I was never so much as to lean against.

Grandma caught him in the back yard drilling holes in her precious willow tree and all she said was, "Don't play with that tool, dear, you might hurt yourself."

Of course, I had let my feelings about this travesty of justice be known from time to time. But all I got from this protest was a shushing and a lecture about how Kenny was upset because they had been in the bombing, had had to leave their home and how he was worried about his father, who had been wounded.

And now, here he was on Christmas Eve talking to me when we were supposed to be asleep. "Didn't you hear what Aunt Winnie said? Santa won't come until we go to sleep," I whispered across the room.

"Do you really think he'll come?" he asked.

"Not if we're awake," I responded.

"He won't bring me anything," he said.

"Why not?" I asked, thinking that perhaps at last he was worried about all the rules he had been breaking. "You don't think that you've been too bad?"

"No, it's just that Santa doesn't know where I am. He thinks that I live in Honolulu. I don't think that he can find me here."

For a moment, I thought Kenny was going to cry. "Hey," I said, remembering what I'd overheard about the fate of some of my presents. "You'll get some presents, don't worry."

"Maybe, but not what I asked Santa for," he said.

"Listen. If Santa knows if we are sleeping or not, he's got to know where we are," I reasoned.

"Yeah," he said, with doubt clear in his answer. "I guess we'd better get to sleep."

"Are you two going to get up or don't you care about what Santa brought?" It was my mother's voice that woke us with a start. We jumped out of bed and would have flown down the stairs but for her insistence that we put on slippers and bathrobes.

"Now don't go wild," she cautioned. "We have several visitors downstairs who expect to see two well-behaved little boys who deserve what Santa has brought them."

"Kenny doesn't think Santa knows where he is," I blurted. "But I told him that Santa knows everything. Isn't that right, Mom?"

Taken aback, my mother hesitated for a moment and then said, "In a moment you'll see for yourself. Now let's walk slowly down the stairs."

For once, Kenny followed instructions and actually took my mother's hand as we were led down the stairs. We both knew what to look for. Santa's presents were unwrapped. The wrapped ones were from family members and maybe for other family members as well as for us. You couldn't tell about them.

But the presents that were unwrapped were for us. Well, maybe just for me, if Santa couldn't find Kenny on the Blacked-Out Christmas. Somehow my worries about what I would get or not get for Christmas became concern for Kenny.

Halfway down I could see that the big room was packed with family and friends all smiling and looking pleased at the sight of us. All waiting expectantly for our reactions to what Santa had brought.

Kenny stopped on the stairs, pulling my mother's arm. I leaned over his head to see what was stopping him. There was the tree, and yes, there were things that I had asked for. To the left of the tree were a ball, bat and glove. Next to them a drum. And, yes, that long box. It must be a fishing pole. Yeah, that's what I wanted most of all.

But wait a moment. What's that on the other side of the tree? Another drum! Another bat, ball and glove. But no fishing pole; I don't see another fishing pole. But look at that, there's a cowboy outfit.

Simultaneously, we threw away all pretense of being well-behaved little boys and charged down the remaining stairs, across the room and to our respective sides of the tree.

Out came the fishing pole, on went the cowboy outfit, and eventually the whole room jingled with joy and laughter as the expectations of the assembled adults were confirmed.

Later, I heard Kenny tell his mother, "Santa knows where everybody is. He must know where Dad is, too."

The next few years found my mother and me following Dad around the country as he pursued his military career in such places as Texas, Mississippi, Alabama, Vermont and different places in California. Never again did I have to worry about a blacked-out Christmas and not once did I worry that Santa wouldn't know where I was. He found me every time.

RELOCATING THE CHILDREN

*where are we when we are not home when we cannot
find our way to places we know and people we love where
is home now where are our parents where are the pets
who love us in their manner of caring for a lifetime
confusion is not comfort is not home is not mother is
not father is not our sisters and brothers or neighbors or
the animals who share our lives we ask questions all day
long all night long we call for the dog we left behind*

In the early days of war in Europe, efforts were made to move masses of children away from areas of highest danger. The results, however, were not always what were anticipated. Many of those children had nearly insurmountable adjustments to make. There were uncertain responses to displacement, worries about their families now far away, fears of never seeing home again, and insecurities about living in unfamiliar surroundings and unsatisfactory conditions. Some children were exploited. Others became restless and rebellious. Of course, not all who were taken from their homes fared poorly. Many were able to continue their educations, have nutritious meals, and live with loving families.

One particular situation, different from other relocation efforts, involved the Jewish children in "Operation *Kindertransport*" from Germany to Great Britain in 1938-39. Both Jews and Christians participated in this effort, saving thousands of youngsters from political and physical persecution. The operation ended when Germany invaded Poland in 1939, but the children who took part were grateful for the generosity of British families who welcomed them into their homes. It was a courageous and loving act of the Jewish parents to send their children to safety, knowing they would likely never be reunited once the war ended. The transported children began their journey by train not only from Berlin, but also from Vienna, Prague, and other major cities. After crossing the Dutch and Belgian borders they were taken by ship to

England. Some children, however, remained in Belgium and Holland, rather than going on. The last ship to leave with children, from Ymuiden, Holland May 14, 1940, carried some 80 children who had initially remained in what they thought to be safety in Holland. But that country fell to the Germans the day the freighter left with its final shipload of escaping children, enduring the frightening experience of having the ship raked by gunfire from German warplanes. It is estimated that approximately 10,000 children, some of them infants, were saved through this effort. Most were Jewish but others also were with them.[9]

Walter Falk was one of the "Kinder," and now lives in Greensboro, NC. In 2007 he was interviewed by Lorraine Ahearn for the Greensboro News & Record, *a story later printed in a Jewish newsletter, and then published in a collection of Ahearn's feature articles in* The Man Who Became Santa Claus and Other Winter Tales. *Falk's story is drawn from her article.*

When Walter Falk left his home in Karlsrühe, Germany, to seek safety in his grandmother's country village, his life was to take a new and strange journey, bringing him eventually to Greensboro, North Carolina. The story began during the events of the infamous *Kristallnacht* in 1938, when Jews were subjected to being forced out of their homes, their storefronts smashed, and heavy restrictions placed on them throughout the country. Walter, 11, and his widowed mother had already been evicted from their nice apartment, and were living over a Jewish shoe store. Walter was sent to a school for Jewish students in makeshift buildings on the grounds of an insane asylum. On November 9, what was to be known as *Kristallnacht* took place. He came home from school to discover the shopwindows of the store below their apartment smashed and the shoes from the store scattered around in the street. He rushed up to their rooms only to find that the Nazis had torn up the apartment, apparently looking for a wall safe behind paintings and curtains. That was enough for his mother to decide that they must leave and go to her parents' home in a country village.

---

[9] http://kindertransport.org/history07_KTAoverview.htm, the website for "KinderTransport and KTA History."

His mother sought unsuccessfully to send him to Palestine, a location encouraged by the Nazi government before the war began. She then learned of the *Kindertransport* program for evacuating Jewish children to Great Britain, and soon afterwards his mother kissed him goodbye as he boarded a train out of Germany. Walter was to reach Holland and cross the English Channel into Great Britain. He did not know then that he would never again see his mother. He corresponded with her by way of a relative in Switzerland until 1942, when the letters from her stopped. She had been taken to the death camp in Auschwitz, Poland, where she died.

In England, Walter was housed in various locations, in hostels and homes for children. Other Jewish children lived with families, and some of those were adopted and remained in England. When Germany invaded Poland in September, 1939, the war began and the *Kindertransport* program ended. Walter was then to endure the Battle of Britain, when German planes bombed the cities and countryside of England. He survived, and after the war emigrated to New York City where his aunt lived. There he met his wife Ginger, who had also escaped Germany as a Jewish child and grew up in Argentina. (She has since died.) He returned to Germany in 1950 as a soldier in the US Army. After his military service he became a salesman, settling in Greensboro, NC. He has never forgotten those in his family who died in concentration camps or under other difficult conditions. In memory of his mother, he has placed a tombstone in the local Jewish cemetery. Following the Jewish custom of laying pebbles on a loved one's tomb to signify that the person is remembered, he selects stones to place on his mother's gravestone even though the ground beneath is empty. They are worn smooth and have been washed clean. He has in this practice kept the memory of his mother alive and honored.

***

British children were evacuated to safer areas in the countryside during 1939-45, following the German invasion of Poland. In these cases, traumatic experiences often resulted. City children had to adjust to rural life. Poor children were uncomfortable in wealthy homes. Some British children were sent far away to the US, Canada, Australia, New Zealand and South Africa.[10] At war's end, other difficult experiences awaited: Some 38,000 British children had been abandoned by their families and listed by local authorities as "unclaimed." Yet in spite of such negative experiences, overall the effects of such relocations were positive, making that generation one of independent people.[11]

Relocated German children, however, comprised "the largest evacuation of children in history."[12] They were sent either to rural areas or to German-occupied countries. As with other children, their experiences were a mixture of good fortune and sorrow. Some of these children were able to remain with their families, all finding refuge in the countryside. Others were sent to government-run camps for indoctrination. On the positive side, they learned to be flexible and independent, but they also received heavy quantities of Hitler Youth and Nazi Party propaganda. For this aspect, teenagers often resented such training, seen as an intrusion and an attempt to control their lives and determine their thought processes. This part of the experience was further worsened by their feelings of powerlessness to resist indoctrination.[13]

In this country, Japanese-American children who lived on the West Coast were experiencing another kind of evacuation. They, along with their families, were being sent to relocation centers and then to camps in various parts of the western states. These children, along with their parents, were considered to be threats to the country solely on the basis of their Japanese background. Eventually, after the end of the war, the detainees were released to return to whatever might remain of their homes. Despite the fact that many young Japanese men volunteered for the military, desiring to prove their loyalty to their country, that time held many disappointments for them. For the young, parting from their homes was sad and bewildering.

---

[10] Werner, *Through the Eyes of Innocents,* 39 ff.

[11] Werner, *Through the Eyes of Innocents,* 48.

[12] Werner, *Through the Eyes of Innocents,* 48.

[13] Werner, *Through the Eyes of Innocents,* 58.

Not easy to declare love of country
when your country rejects you and your kind.
Innocence sits in the lap of Protection
yet betrayed by this outrage. Who can
be free in a homeland that denies
one's right to be accepted equally?
Who are those who come to these shores
and then refuse entrance to the latecomers,
to those who look like the enemy?

War is difficult for families anywhere, but for those of Japanese descent, the problems encountered at that time were enlarged beyond what we might imagine in our own time. Fears were commonly expressed that Japanese living in the United States, even those who were citizens, would feel a primary loyalty to Japan and therefore attempt to bring harm to this country. It was a false fear. Japanese soldiers in the US military distinguished themselves in their service to their country, the country of all US citizens. Those least responsible for any kind of threat were of course the children, innocent and afraid, insecure after their home life had been disrupted. We can hope that this kind of treatment to our own citizens will never again happen on our own soil and initiated by our own government.

Incarceration of the Innocents speaks its own evil: Security and fear
are partners with the power of governments. Hysteria. Japanese
can't be trusted. Even those who have been here for generations.
Put them in camps far away from good Americans. Take the children
away from all their known security. Leave the family dog standing
abandoned at the gated fence. Leave for unknown, unimagined
separation and structures of life. A drop of alien blood? Take the
child away. Take the parents away. Take freedom away. Then
apologize 50 years later when we have forgotten but they carry the
indelible pain of loss, suspicion, contempt ...marked forever.

THE DARK OF WAR

There are no dividing lines really
and the ones who stay at home
all of them ripped from the familiar
and forced out of the sequential life
that measured their days, like some
untimely birth into torment.
Hell would be an improvement.

No matter what part of the world a child lived in during the war, there were repercussions. Some lived outside the battle lines while others faced constant terror and violence. Those directly in war zones or the surrounding countryside learned the lessons of loss and sacrifice, of hunger and danger. In spite of its being against their will, this experience was unavoidable. Not only were they made aware of the military losses, including those within their families, but also of those who played no part in warfare. One chronicler of the experiences of children comments:

The children of World War II learned to mourn the loss of civilian lives as well. Among the first to lose close family members were Polish children who had been deported from their homes between the spring of 1940 and the summer of 1941. Some 140,000 youngsters were sent with their families by truck and train to the Taiga, a 1,000-mile belt of forests stretching right across Europe and Asia, from the White Sea to the Pacific Ocean. There they were forcibly settled in labor camps. After a short, scorching hot summer, they experienced nine months of winter, with temperatures as low as 90 degrees below zero. They were constantly hungry and cold.

[The writer illustrates those ordeals by the tragic account of a woman and her son, frozen to death on a sleigh when they had gone out to exchange clothing

for food in the nearby villages.][14]

In spite of all the reasons for children to be traumatized by the horrors of war, youthful resilience endured and resourcefulness took over. Games and competitions managed to be daily routines when life became even more difficult because of bombings and blackouts and all manner of things which can frighten children as well as adults. Instead of collecting baseball cards or gum wrappers, both British and German children scoured the rubble following air attacks, looking for interesting pieces of metal, shrapnel from anti-aircraft guns or bomb fragments. The children's collections grew in size, along with their ability to recognize what country the scraps came from: America, Great Britain, France, Germany. The children had become experts on the leftover scraps of warfare.[15]

> *Trademarks, brand names, manufactured identity*
> *take on new challenges. Can you guess the country?*
> *Try out this missile for style and ease of destruction.*
> *We teach them early to learn who's who and what's*
> *what. Some day this knowledge will serve them well.*

The wisdom of a five-year-old saved his life following the bombing raid which hit his London home. He knew that miners buried in an accident would sing in order for search crews to find them. He could hear sounds around him of search parties but was unable to tap on anything to indicate his presence. He remembered the miners, and began singing, "the only song I knew."[16]

> *Just a thin sound from somewhere. We couldn't make out*
> *where in the rubble it was. A familiar tune. Yes, that's it,*
> *a tiny pitch barely there: "God save our gracious king . . ."*
> *flashlight beams find the small body framed beneath the fallen*

---

[14] Werner, *Through the Eyes of Innocents,* 170.
[15] Werner, *Through the Eyes of Innocents,* 19.
[16] Werner, *Through the Eyes of Innocents,* 20.

timbers. Our team recognizes the small but wide eyes, mirroring
terror, betraying fear, yes, the neighbor's boy.
Unearth him. Carry him out. Lazarus out from the tomb he is.

Elsewhere violence entered lives in rural areas as well as in urban. Those in outlying areas were least prepared for the assault on their homeland. It may have been in the form of invading soldiers in tanks shooting purposely to frighten a helpless populace. Or perhaps innocent families in conquered territories were caught by bombing raids from friendly aircraft, sending death indiscriminately. Indelible scenes are forever imprinted on memories of children, of blankets covering bodies of classmates and teachers. Of the face of the enemy bearing a cold and distant regard. War brings together common moments of stunned recognition of unexpected danger.

In Norway, under German control, the British sent bombing raids to destroy the military positions there. Damage from the attacks, however, affected the Norwegian people who were non-combatants. Falling bombs do not always discriminate between the enemy and the ally. When a school received a misdirected bomb in one town, the disaster was never erased from the people's memories, as children and teachers were killed by this unintended consequence.[17]

side by side
row after row
small still forms
beneath the blankets
in the classroom of death
where teachers plan
new lessons
what do we learn

There were always those situations that seem incongruous with the purpose of life. In war the destruction of life destroys any purpose that might have existed. The survivors of such devastation are marked with

---

[17] Tore Iversen, *Children of the Storm: Childhood Memories of World War I*, 14.

undeniable memories that cannot always be stored into the mind's oblivion, but instead insist on returning uninvited into one's life later. The darkest moments for those not on the battle lines operate in contradiction to any noble cause that soldiers at the front might maintain. These dark moments haunt the spirit forever.

In Czechoslovakia (now the Czech Republic), a Jewish girl witnessed her grandfather's suicide after he received his summons to be deported to a concentration camp. Taking poison, this man who as a doctor had saved the lives of others made his private "final solution." In light of what has been reported about the concentration camps, one wonders that his decision was perhaps the most generous act of all for his family. Nevertheless, it was a memory she carried with her the remainder of her life.[18]

> *Is it worse to die by one's own hand*
> *or by the power of those who control*
> *our fate? There is honor either way,*
> *for one is a protest against inhumanity*
> *and the other is inhumanity itself.*
> *Was the God of war present,*
> *or a God who suffered?*

The plight of the Jews in the Warsaw ghettos was as frightening as that in Czechoslovakia. They lived in fear of the German soldiers who sought those in hiding in order to send them to concentration camps. Every aspect of the former life in the ghetto had changed, and the ones sought after lived like animals watching for the hunters. Certain death would come, sooner or later. There were many stories of the hunted, of some who almost inexplicably survived the searches and fled for refuge in neighboring countries. Survivors told their stories as lessons for others, to be certain that the horrors of the Holocaust would never again take place.[19]

---

[18] Hana Rehakova, *Children of the Storm*, 60.
[19] Stefanie Seltzer, newspaper feature, Greensboro *News & Record*, 9/2/07, B1, B3.

Nothing is permanent anymore.
Stay one day, one week, then on
to new hiding places. Run, children,
run. Sssshhh. Family disappears,
one by one. Friends disappear.
The time disappears, reappears
where dreams are hiding.

The Germans set about to liquidate the Lödz Ghetto as the Russians neared Warsaw in 1944. Lists were compiled of those to send away to death camps. Exceptions were made for any who were considered essential to the German factories there. These were spared the fate, for the time being, of their family members.[20]

We are considered necessary
because we work hard in this factory
turning out products for death machines.
Others, of course, being so young, have
little value for what serves power.
We don't see them here anymore.

Even youth in their teens were called on to serve. Some cared for the wounded in Warsaw's hospitals. This work was frustrating because of the lack of sufficient medical supplies. In many cases, one could provide nothing but comfort, or carry water and equipment. The terrible wounds suffered by the Home Army were evident in loss of sight or limbs or mental capacities. At times there was no way to serve except to listen.[21]

the gift to listen
is a generous one
for what is left to do
when all else fails ...

---

[20] Jacob Moses Kusmierski, *Children of the Storm,* 77-79.
[21] Magdalena Abakanowicz, *Children of the Storm,* 62.

what remains of a body
on the stretcher
talks

Russians endured tremendous suffering when the German armies invaded their country. The young, however, did what they could. One choice for the older ones was to join the partisan underground behind the enemy lines. Acts of bravery were common, even when the result was death.[22]

This is a time when the young should
go on picnics, visit school friends
share secrets, read novels.
This is not a time to fire submachine guns
nor kill enemies nor be killed.
What monstrous demon presides
over a time such as this?
The corpses of the young see nothing.

German soldiers in Norway were placed in local homes until a military fort could be built to house anti-aircraft artillery. Once that construction was complete, residents suffered doubly: From the prior intrusions into their homes, and also from English air attacks near the end of the war which were targeting the anti-aircraft artillery. These dangers were multiplied at the time of the German retreat from Russian troops crossing the border. As a final act, the German military burned houses, killed livestock, and drove local residents away.[23]

timber burns quickly when it houses
a lifetime of family, enduring as history
fragile as a whiff of smoke
so much there to spark the flames
so little really that goes
because in the ashes we find our memory

---

[22] Werner, the story of Ina Konstantinova, *Through the Eyes of Innocents*, 62.
[23] Grete Eliassen, *Children of the Storm*, 63-64.

Schools in England remained open in spite of the air attacks. Yet there were instructions on what to do in the event of a raid. A high school student in those days remembers still a particular incident: "The rule was that if the air-raid siren went off we had to run home, because there was not an air-raid shelter at school. So one day the siren sounded and we were running home when I heard the sound of a German fighter plane. I glanced up and there it was, coming right at us, machine guns firing. I lay flat as possible between the sidewalk and road. The plane passed over us. Later on we heard that a plane had been shot down, maybe the one firing on us. The school decided to put an air-raid shelter under the school yard after that incident."[24]

it is the siren call
not the bell that tolls
the end of class
today's assignment:
dash for home
the goal is shelter
we pass the course this time

A most graphic and disturbing image, which impels one to decry all forms of violence, occurred in Okinawa. Writing about her ordeals as a seven-year-old Japanese girl fleeing from American forces and avoiding Japanese military, Tomika Higa remembers her long journey across the island. In her book about that terrifying time, she describes how she and several siblings began searching for their father, believed to be alive somewhere. On their way, they came across a scene never forgotten. They saw a baby trying to nurse his dead mother, blood smeared across his face, reaching out to the horrified children for help.[25]

---

[24] Eileen D. Morman, personal account, Greensboro, NC. (more complete story included later in the book)

[25] Tomiko Higa, *The Girl with the White Flag*, 48.

Those medieval paintings by the great artists of Europe:
the serenity of the holy woman with her holy Child
nursing her infant with a holy love, protective
and nourishing, the placid infant at her breast content
and biding time until his brutal death, is no image
for this dead mother and her infant
on the abandoned battlefield. This time,
life-giving milk for the child of her womb is replaced
with the mother's very blood, painting that small face
not with serenity but as witness to terror
beyond comprehension. The baby is marked forever
by absence of fulfillment and expectation.
What have we done?

Hail Mary, who lies beneath
the bloodied soil.

A view from the other side

What follows is an excerpt from a journal kept by Ernst Albrecht, who served for a week near the end of the war helping his father, a physician in Bremen serving with the German Medical Corps. The introductory section is written by his younger sister, Adelheid Albrecht Haas, who translated this piece, with the help of others, for inclusion in this book. Adelheid and I began our friendship during our first year at Randolph-Macon Woman's College, when she was an exchange student that year, and have maintained it over the years since. This story from her brother's journal is perhaps the most moving of all the personal accounts I have recorded.

Two Days in the Diary of a German Boy, April 1945

Introduction by Adelheid Albrecht Haas:
Our family house was situated in the centre of Bremen. During the war, British bombers had to cross the region when they set course for

other German cities such as Berlin or Dresden. As a result, the wailing of sirens was a frequent occurrence, at times almost daily and nearly every night. Then we had to leave the house immediately and run to the next air-raid shelter while the anti-aircraft guns were already firing into the sky. In the shelter we spent many hours. Most of the times the planes just flew past Bremen, but on several occasions, when we were able to leave the shelter, the sky glowed red with burning houses. Miraculously, our house was not hit by a bomb, but the neighbouring houses were and burnt down.

I don't remember being very much afraid because our mother always was with us children. In the shelter she told us stories and her calm voice inspired strength and hope. Our father, a doctor, was captain of a medical unit. The men administered first-aid to the wounded during and after air-raids. When the air raids became so dangerous that schools were closed and people evacuated, my mother and my three brothers and I moved to a weekend cottage in the country, where we could feel relatively safe. My father stayed in town and took care of his patients and the wounded after an air-raid.

Like all German boys at the time, my older brothers belonged to the youth organization called the *Hitlerjugend*. Membership was compulsory but nevertheless, my brothers enjoyed the comradeship with other boys. We all loved our *Heimat* (homeland) and were convinced that German soldiers fought for a just cause. Only censored information was transmitted by radio and newspapers, so we did not have an objective picture of what really happened.

Towards the end of the war, men who were too old for active fighting, as well as 16-year-old boys, were recruited for anti-tank units. My brother Ernst, born on 29 June, 1930, lying about his age, volunteered in March, 1945 for membership in such a unit. He wanted to defend his homeland. When our father realized this he strictly forbade his son such a dangerous adventure, adding however, "I promise you will get the opportunity to serve your country."

In April, 1945, my brother Ernst joined my father's medical unit and took part in caring for the wounded after an air raid. The following text is an abbreviated version of what Ernst wrote on May 1 in his diary.

Monday, April 24 1945

All day long bombs were falling thick as carpets. At 2:30 p.m. we got the order for action: Go to *Regensburger Schule* (a school). Immediately we got ready, Papa, I and three more men, in a word, the emergency team. Papa and Mr. Schinke sat in the front of the car, the rest of us in the back with our first-aid supply, more on top of than next to each other, steel helmets on our heads. It was eerie, uneasy, but at the same time alarmingly quiet, the air almost sultry and oppressive in spite of heavy rain. I was restive but I was not afraid. On the contrary, I was glad, proud and glad, that I could risk my life. At last I could cast not just my thoughts and words but also my strength and my life onto the scales of war. If death would have come this moment, in whatever form, I would have died without complaint, proud and content!

Suddenly the air roared, the earth trembled, then thunder, crashing, roaring. An immense cloud of sand, mortar, wood and stones mounted into the air 200 or 300 meters high. The first carpet of bombs only 400 meters away. Unwavering, we drove on. I didn't feel fright, only powerlessness in the face of fate. Everywhere blocked streets, damaged bridges, but now we are there.

We leave the car and enter the school. Policemen receive us, their faces marked by the mad horror of the last hours. My first action! Near the door a captain is lying; his left leg is completely cut off. The leg lies loose in the trouser leg. His face is ashen, his hands are pale, his hair full of mortar. Papa checks his pulse. "We cannot help him anymore!" A few feet away an old woman is lying. Dead! Her hair is scattered on the floor. We are standing on a carpet of hair. I don't understand how this could have happened. A rotten stink rises – dreadful!

We head for the cellar. Out of the uncanny black depth we hear groaning, uncontrolled weeping, whimpering of agonized pain. Alas! And the smell of blood – I feel dizzy. Papa gives me a candle, which I light without saying a word. Then we descend. The candle burns flickeringly. A cold shudder passes my back; silently I press my teeth together. Everybody is silent except for the wounded. We look around in the dismal, stinking chamber of death and try to distinguish between living and dead. First of all we attend a woman with a dreadful wound in the back which severed her spine. Whimpering, tormented, she asks for help: "Doctor, give me an injection so that I can die quickly. Please do, dear Doctor! It is not a sin. I must die anyway! Please, dear Doctor, an injection!" Then a tormented cry: "The pain! Help me! An injection! It is no sin!" Oh, we are transient humans, powerless worms, just balls in the game of fate! Papa inspects the wound and injects morphine, the whimpering stops, death stands on the threshold – waiting! I feel close to vomiting, and passing the dead, run upstairs. Fresh air! Outside the rain is pouring. I'm feeling better, but the crying and groaning will not leave my ears. With one of our men we patrol the adjacent streets looking for the wounded. We ask everybody: "Where are the wounded?" Most of them just look at us with mad and anxious eyes, not saying anything, and hurry on without a destination or a plan. They pass through the ruins, living, walking, horrible witnesses of the bombing terror. Pale, trembling fear is reflected on every face! Back in the school we report to papa, who takes care of the wounded, assisted by the untiring Mr. Schinke. Suddenly the watch on the roof cries: "Attention! New airplanes!" Everybody rushes into the cellar, me, too! I, as well as the others, am carried away with the panic. Again the roaring in the air. A dreadful crash! A bomb hits our school. Stones, glass and mortar fly around; an irresistible draft presses us against the wall. Then it is over; we continue our work.

The first ambulance cars arrive. Men with stretchers enter; with infinite care the wounded are transported – but only the most seriously wounded! Papa and I are taking care of a woman whose leg is almost completely severed at the knee. At the lightest touch she cries with pain until we have dressed the gaping wound, put the woman on the stretcher and applied a tourniquet to the leg!

I will not go into details, the horrible faces of the dead, the attempts to get the names of the helpless creatures, etc. After a while we leave the cellar and go to a subterranean air-raid shelter about twenty meters away, which was also hit by a bomb. On the way, people gather around us: "Where is the doctor? I must see the doctor!" Every one of them has a request. Some are wounded, others have a message: "In the next street a woman is lying, who lost her arm. She is bleeding to death!"

We enter the bunker, descend into the dark, gaping depth. Again death is our guide! Right at the door two seriously wounded are lying. I will not describe the injuries, or the bloody work, which we have to do. No more! It was terrible. With a candle we grope in the dark through narrow corridors, trying not to step on wounded persons. It was the same as in the school. I just can't tell any more about it.

I was surprised, however, that I could stand all this much better than before. At least loathing didn't choke so painfully in my throat and my stomach. When all the wounds were dressed, Papa returned to the school and left me to supervise the transport of the wounded. I was hugely relieved when all of them were in the ambulance and I could go outside into the refreshing rain.

Back to the school. I was standing at the side of the dead captain who had lost his leg, when I saw a young girl looking around. She approached me. When she saw the dead man, she cried in a terribly forced voice: "My father!" She threw her arms up and ran away crying insanely. Shall I cry the same words one of the next days?

Papa comes and shakes me out of my stupor: "Make sure that all wounded are carried out of this room!" "Yes, Papa!" At last it is done. We can leave the terrible mortuary. It is 9:30 p.m. Five hours full of blood, five hours full of misery. All the time I had not once looked at my watch. Now it is dark. Exhausted, we arrive at the hospital. The corridors are full of wounded. Here too groaning and whimpering. Here too the loathing of blood. Nurse Anna offers us something to eat. But I cannot eat, not yet. First of all I wash at the pump. I must get rid of the blood on my body. It is revolting. I take care not to touch my face with my hands, even after having them cleaned. Then hunger sets in. We cut some slices of bread and eat, our eyes still on the wounded. In front of us a young girl is sitting with an infant in her arms. The child has a fractured skull and cries incessantly. The girl sobs: "He is not baptized." The minister hears her words and among the wounded he administers the baptism. When the holy ritual is completed the crying stops. The child is dead. The girl cries convulsively. Now she is completely alone. Her little brother is dead, her father and mother have lost their lives under a bomb. Who will take care of her now – without a house, without money, without bread?

I am exhausted, but there is no hope of sleep. At 2:00 a.m. I can lie down on a 30 cm. wide bench at the door of the operation theatre. I only take off my heavy boots, cover myself with a blanket, put another one under my head and try to sleep. Every fifteen minutes I have to change the position because the hard bench hurts. I have wild dreams, cannot get rid of the pictures of the day: The terrible wounds, the cries, the faces of the dead, the carpets of bombs! At 6 o'clock I cannot stand it any longer. I get up, wash my face and hands at the pump outside. After the incessant bombarding during the night it is almost quiet for the first time. Papa is awake, too. He seems to have slept well on the operating table. Slowly he puts on his boots. A new day begins.

Tuesday, April 25

At nine o'clock fighting began again, the same as the day before. The air-raid shelter of the hospital was packed, only pale light, and as the ventilator wasn't working, there was an oppressive, suffocating air, a terrible smell of the operating theatre (where we had slept before) and a constantly mounting heat. Dirty, perspiring, tired and with a dry throat I stood in the corridor during the first hours. Later I found a place at a table and dozed for hours. I no longer took notice of the bombs. Most of the time Papa was at the headquarters.

At noon we visited the wounded. I was surprised to see that they looked much better than yesterday. Without doubt the immediate help given by Papa saved the lives of many, chiefly because they could be operated on so soon.

At two o'clock the next order for action: *Bunker Osterfeuerbergstrasse*! It is situated in the same region as yesterday. Our emergency squad starts immediately. Unhindered, we reach the damaged place. Dead persons everywhere in the streets. We just make sure, in case anyone is still alive, then we go on. The dead must wait, the wounded come first. But we didn't find any. We went into every house. All were without life, empty, devastated. I cried: "Hallo, is anyone there?" No answer! Only the echo of my own words. Carefully I mounted a stair. The building could collapse any moment, then help me God! I looked into every room, but nowhere a living soul, only devastation. It was strange; I still was afraid to look into the glassy eyes of a dead person. I froze every time I came across a dead body unexpectedly.

In every house it is the same. When everything is checked we meet again. Someone comes running: "In the house over there they have found two!" We go there. Two women! One of them is dead, her face contorted by pain. The other has wounds on hand and jaw. Her lips and the jaw are split open. The flesh can be seen, not bleeding any more. Papa inspects the wound and leaves it up to Schinke and me to dress the wounds. We carry the woman into a house and take care of her. Then Schinke takes out of his pocket a small bottle of red wine and gives me some. This sign of comradeship pleases me more than the wine.

In front of us a house is standing on fire. Two *Hitlerjugend* try to extinguish the fire. Suddenly a thundering noise; the house collapses. A shower of stones comes down on them. I think, "two more dead," but a miracle: Unhurt they jump away. Nobody can say that no guardian angels exist! But nobody should believe that it was quiet. Incessantly low-flying planes roared overhead. Every few minutes shells screamed and exploded with loud cracks. But we didn't take notice any more. Everybody is powerless against fate!

When the wounded were carried into the ambulance cars there was time for the dead. We inspected every one, looked for identification cards in the bloody garments. The death certificates were written and put between the pale fingers. Every dead body had to carry its own death certificate! Can you imagine that?

At five o'clock we returned to the hospital, dead tired, dirty, covered with blood – the same as yesterday! All evening I sat at the table. I couldn't get rid of the pictures. I had only one thought: "I must and I will get over this!" Wounded were brought all the time. A girl from the Red Cross worked here. Never before had I seen such a heroic girl. Without fear, she worked like the men!

After supper Papa came: "Now what do you say about the war?" "I am sick of the war!" "Don't you think it is enough now?" "No, I didn't come to leave now." "You have done enough. The enemy is on the outskirts of town. It would be crazy to stay. Probably we won't survive. Do you really think that both of us should die? What about Mami?" "I don't know. I'll think about it this night."

Afterword by Adelheid Albrecht Haas:

The next morning our father and the minister were able to convince Ernst to leave Bremen and join us in the country. After two more days Bremen was occupied by British forces. Papa survived. The experience of these days and the painful process of learning what had happened during the war to people in other countries made an impact on Ernst's life. He became deeply convinced: This must never, ever happen again! After a while he took responsibility in a newly-founded youth organization, *Die Bündishche Jugend* (somewhat like Boy Scouts). As a student he spent a year on a scholarship at Cornell University in Ithaca, NY. After taking a degree in economics at the University of Bonn, he joined the European Coal and Steel Community in Luxembourg and worked there and later at the European Union in Brussels for a united Europe. In 1970, he and his family returned to Germany, where he was elected a member of the *Niedersächsische Landtag* (Lower Saxony State Legislature) and served his country as *Ministerpräsident von Niedersachsen* (Premier of Lower Saxony) from 1976 to 1990.

In Denmark

Life in Denmark was not as intensely traumatic as in other parts of Europe. The Danes, however, were deeply affected by the war, especially by the presence of the German military, which occupied the country after the invasion in 1940.

Karen Wagner was the daughter of Axel Hieronymus Zeuthen, a Lutheran pastor in the Danish state church. She describes her experience of growing up during the war in a family of seven brothers and sisters. After the death of her mother, the family moved from Copenhagen to Aulum, a small village in Jutland, while Karen was still a young child. The rural environment represented a contrast to the city life of Copenhagen, especially the lack of easy access to higher education. In Aulum her widowed father married a local school teacher and Karen's older siblings eventually returned to Copenhagen to further their education at the university. Karen herself later pursued training as an occupational therapist and moved to Basel, Switzerland, where she was employed at the University Hospital. In Basel she met her future husband, a young American student pursuing a doctoral degree in theology at the municipal university. She now lives in North Carolina. Her account of life in Denmark during the war years follows.

On April 9, 1940, the Germans invaded Denmark. "Achtung! Achtung!" sounded loudly from the radio. The sky was full of airplanes. In Copenhagen harbor, cargo ships, usually loaded with coal for Danish factories and homes, revealed German troops instead, hidden in the ships. And there were German tanks everywhere, even in the little village of Aulum, where my family lived. With nearly 400 troops in the village, the Germans lodged themselves in the Fellowship Community Hall and most of the village school building. Just one classroom was left for the students, who had to pass two German guards with guns, in order to get into the school.

We were ordered to have everything dark at night: No streetlights, and black paper blinds covered the windows, to prevent light from being seen outside. I recall going in the evening – and it gets dark very early in the winter – to get fresh milk from a nearby farm. My twin sister and I would go in the middle of the street, singing "A Mighty Fortress Is Our God," thinking the German soldiers would recognize it and not harm us.

There soon was rationing of all food and clothing, and some things we could not get at all: Just one pair of pants or one dress and a pair of shoes for a year! Heat was rationed and we had to burn *Brunkul and tørv*, poor qualities of heating materials that gave off bad odors when burning. Trucks would use wood, or even pine cones, as fuel.

Aulum is located only 40 miles from the west coast of Jutland and the North Sea, facing England. At one point the Germans were intent on attacking England. Almost every day we watched planes fly overhead with bombs ready to attack London. We tried to count the planes flying towards England, and again when they returned, to see if there were fewer returning. That would mean planes had been shot down by the British!

At that time, the Germans were even preparing for a possible invasion by the British, and so they would dig foxholes in our back yards and climb up in our old trees to watch the road going east from the North Sea!

One Saturday night late, my father was preparing his sermon. He heard a noise at the door and found a German officer who had seen a sliver of light in the window and thought it might be the manse next to the church. He wanted to talk to a clergyman, and had tried to get in the church, but was unable to shoot out the lock of the very thick old church door.

My father, a Danish officer in his youth, asked the German to put down his weapon. The man related how sad and upset he was. He was from Austria, and had been forced to join the German army. His wife and daughter were sent to a labor camp in France and he did not know where they were. My father's German was poor, but they prayed the Lord's Prayer together. The next day, the Germans came to get the officer's gun, and said he had been sent to the Eastern Front, which was in Russia and was almost a certain death sentence for the officer.

As the war went on, the Danes started underground groups and picked up secret supplies and weapons, delivered at night by parachutes from British planes. Others were involved in writing underground newspapers to keep the Danes informed. Some others worked on direct sabotage of the railroad systems, to disrupt German troop transports. It is said that such was the case when the Germans were sending troops from Norway through Denmark to fight the Battle of the Bulge. The troops were held back in Denmark by the railroad sabotage, which may have influenced the outcome of that battle.

My older cousin was very active in the Resistance Movement. Those involved in that listened every evening to the radio broadcasts from England, to hear the code messages about the parachute drops. Once in awhile my cousin would take a bunch of parachutes to my aunt and uncle to burn in the furnace, to hide the evidence from the Germans.

We experienced the railroad derailments first hand. The saboteurs derailed a German transport train on a curve right outside our village. They just "moved" the rails in the curve a few inches. The pressure of the train tipped the railroad cars over so that they fell to both sides of the track. I was then older, going to school in the city 16 miles away, and had to use the same railroad, and there was only one track. So we had to stay at home for a couple of days until the track was repaired. Sometimes we rode our bikes to get to school, but they had hard rubber tires on them and it was not comfortable to ride them any distance.

One event brought the various divisions of the underground together.

The Gestapo, with specific orders from Hitler, ordered that all Jews in Denmark were to be "relocated," in this case sent to the concentration camp at Theresienstadt. This was to take place on the evening of the Jewish New Year Celebration in the fall of 1943, when most Jews could be found either in the synagogue or celebrating at home. But the Jews were warned by a high German official from the German consulate of the planned action. During the next two weeks, with organized help from the Danish Resistance Movement and from ordinary Danes, the Jews were able to go first to fishing villages along the coastline, and then were smuggled to safety in Sweden, which was a neutral country. At the time, about 8000 Jews lived in Denmark, and only about 460 were rounded up by the Nazis. (We learned later that there was pressure on the officials at Theresienstadt to provide humane treatment to those 460 sent there, and after the war, some 400 survived and returned to Denmark.) During the absence of the Jews from Denmark, the Danish Ministry of Social Justice took care of their homes and businesses. Neighbors watched over Jewish pets and tended Jewish gardens. Torahs were kept in safety, some even in a Lutheran church. There was very little stealing or looting of any kind involving property belonging to the Jews.

This Danish quality of human decency may have been catching. In statements discovered later, it was revealed that this all would not have been possible if the Germans, even some members of the Gestapo, had not to a certain degree looked the other way rather than obey orders concerning the Jews.

On May 4, 1945, the war in Europe was over, and the Danes were very happy to get all the Germans out of their country.

In The War But At A Distance

The son of an Army surgeon, Jim Matternes describes life during the war years, which began while his family was in Panama. Life for military families was affected by the war in diverse ways. His father, by some stroke of fate or fortune, narrowly missed being in the midst of the early consequences of the Japanese attack, but the family experienced later disruptions caused by the war. I knew his younger brother Jay when we both lived at Ft. Lewis, Washington. Here, Jim recalls the family's wartime experience.

During the decade of the '30's, Army officers were required to serve overseas for designated periods of time. My dad had served one tour of duty in the Philippines, and because it had been a good experience, in 1939 he requested a return to that post with the Medical Corps. The illness of my mom's father, however, caused him to choose an assignment nearer to the United States, and he requested to be sent to Panama. Thus we were spared imprisonment by the Japanese when the war began, and my father perhaps was spared from being on that infamous Bataan Death March, when great numbers of American military men died during that ordeal.

[Ed. Note: My father also almost chose to be assigned to the Philippines instead of Hawaii. He had served once in Hawaii in the late '20's, and thought it would be good to have a variety of experiences in the Pacific area. Fortunately, however, his decision was to return to Hawaii where he and the family had enjoyed the islands earlier. I had not yet been born during that first assignment in Honolulu. Jim Matternes' story continues below.]

Our family, my dad and mom, my younger brother and I re-located to Panama. My dad's assignment was as a surgeon at Gorgas Hospital. It was on the Pacific side of the Canal Zone, and our house was located on a high hill, with the approaches of the Canal at a distance. Two years later, in 1941, we noticed a middle-aged man who constantly showed up on the road there on the hill. He would sit on the guard rail for hours, watching the entrance of the Canal. Below us maybe half a mile, on the Panama City limits, was the German embassy building. We drew our own conclusions about the connection, figuring he was a German spy.

In 1940 and '41, the Army operated minelayer boats that laid mines at the entrance of the Canal. They operated from Ft. Amador. My father and I would often fish on the pier there, and I remember well one night when we were fishing at the end of the pier. From the darkness of the Canal channel we heard British voices but could see nothing. The shore on the opposite side had a leper colony, and we always saw their lights. Then, slowly, something cut off those lights from our view. A completely darkened ship was passing. After that the lights returned gradually. A ship was headed for the Canal, leaving the Pacific side. We could only guess that it was a British ship.

The Panama City limits and the US Canal Zone were separated by a street. When the Germans overran the French in Europe, the German flag with the swastika was proudly flown at the Panama City embassy. When we kids rode past it, we hissed.

On the afternoon of December 7, 1941, we were at Ft. Amador Officers' Beach for a swim. Suddenly the loudspeaker came on announcing that all officers report immediately to their posts, because of an emergency. What happened? We had no idea. We were to learn that the Japanese had attacked the naval base at Pearl Harbor, on the Hawaiian island of Oahu.

When the news of the attack reached the Canal Zone, an interesting story began to play itself out. It seems that ammunition had been stored in the jungle, and the soldiers were quickly taken from their barracks and put on trucks to retrieve the ammunition. Some of the soldiers undertook this assignment dressed only in their underwear, as they were not given time even to dress before leaving on the trucks for the jungle.

The next day at school, kids were coming in a couple of hours late and the teacher asked why. The answer was unexpected: In Panama City, police were picking up anyone who looked German, Italian, or Japanese, kids included. Those detained were taken to a camp at a determined location, enclosed in a fence, and given a pile of wood to build their own shelter. They refused until one of our heavy rain storms convinced them to cooperate.

There had been a time before the attack on Pearl Harbor when kids from Army bases were given gas masks to wear all the time. My brother Jay and I were upset that we didn't get them. The masks were a response to the gassing in World War I by the Germans, so as to be prepared in case of a similar action in the next war.

Shortly after that attack, Dad and Mom decided to go to the movies at Ft. Clayton. It was night time, and there was a guard at the gate, nervous and shaky, holding a loaded .45 pistol, checking ID's. My dad was very concerned that the guard might do something irrational. It was a time when the whole area was living on a bundle of nerves.

Even before the Pearl Harbor event, the Canal was on high alert. A merchant ship was in one of the locks. A crewman went on deck, threw a couple of beer cans into the lock, and the lock was shut down until the cans were found. The fear had been that the beer cans had instead been bombs.

At this time also, no German, Italian or Japanese ship was in the Canal system, and hadn't been for several days before Pearl Harbor was attacked. Months before that, an Italian passenger ship was in the Canal system, and was seized and held for the British. The crew had cut the propeller shaft, to eliminate easy capture by the British. And they were successful, because the British had to tow the ship away, a difficult endeavor, rather than send it to England under its own power.

During the middle of 1941, before the Japanese attack, my folks were acquainted with a Navy chaplain. He was re-assigned to duty at Pearl Harbor, and as was the practice at that time, his group was transported by ship. It came through the canal and docked on the Pacific side, which allowed time for a day or two of visits before the ship headed off to Pearl Harbor. Once they arrived, the officers were housed in quarters which were lined up in a row. At the time of the Japanese attack, planes shot up the houses, but the one housing our chaplain friend, located in the middle of that row, was the only one not hit by bullets. We puzzled over possible reasons when we heard the news, but could not find a rational explanation. So the question of *why?* remains.

A tragic incident occurred while we were still in Panama after the war began, involving a family we knew. Another medical officer and his family were close friends with my parents. They had a daughter, and she and I became very attached to each other in that "puppy love" stage. Then her dad was sent to the Pacific, where he made visits to various hospitals. He went to the different sites in a light plane heavily marked with red crosses. A Japanese airman shot the plane down, and the doctor's remains were found, reduced to nothing but ashes.

In January of 1942, families of American military personnel in Panama were evacuated after 30 days' notice. Soldiers came to crate our furniture. Mom, Jay and I were transported to Cristobal, on the Atlantic side, and put on a recently-occupied troop ship. That Friday before departure, I said my farewells to schoolmates. On Monday morning I met one of the schoolmates on the dock. He had been given only 48 hours' notice. Dad remained in the Canal Zone for another year. When he finally got a ship to the USA, the feeling was that the ship was being chased by German subs.

Our return to the States brought us to New Orleans. During the journey the ship was blacked out at night. Up forward during the day, a civilian was on duty, ready to fire ground light-weight cannons. He sat with them all during the daylight hours. At night, Mom pushed the curtains to the porthole aside, and opened it to allow air into the stateroom. At some time one night, my brother Jay apparently dropped a toy through it onto the deck and got out of bed and turned on the room light. Panic ensued, because he could have tipped off a sub watching for signs of American ships. But we were again in luck: No torpedo!

The ship docked at New Orleans, and because we were fresh from the hot tropics and were dressed accordingly, we felt frozen in the winter chill we encountered there. For a couple of years after that I had bouts of pneumonia which were attributed to the sudden cold exposure when we came to a much colder climate than there had been in Panama.

During the war later, Dad was assigned to duty in England and had a couple of hospitals under his command. At night, he would watch Hitler's buzz bombs coming into England. One blew out the end of one of his hospitals. The rest of our family lived with my maternal grandfather, also an MD, for the war years. My sister was born while Dad was in England. Victory gardens were the rage at the time, and I had mine where a plot of land had been set aside. I rode my bike to and from it, as I took care of the garden.

At the end of the war in Europe, Dad returned to the USA and was assembling a unit to head for the Japanese conflict. The atomic bomb attacks on Japan changed that possibility and we ended up instead at Ft. Lewis, Washington.

A Dutch Experience In Java And Australia

Claire Koster was living in Java when the war began in the Pacific region. Her father, from Holland, first worked for the Dutch government there, when Java was part of the Dutch East Indies. Subsequently he worked for a private industry there, and married a Hungarian woman who was living in Java. Following a brief time back in Holland, the family returned to Southeast Asia in

1936, living in Singapore where her uncle was in business. Some years later, she came to the United States by virtue of having worked with Honeywell in Amsterdam after the war, making it possible for her to obtain a visa. She married an American soon after and was able to become a citizen. She lives in Clemmons, NC, near Winston-Salem. The following are excerpts from the account of her life during the war years, with slight editing.

With World War II threatening to close in on us, in 1940 it was decided to ship everything to Australia, sell the business and sit out the war. My aunt and uncle went on ahead to Australia, and my mother took me to Perth and put me in boarding school (Presbyterian Ladies College). She waited for my father to come, but he procrastinated, and she finally went back to Singapore to get him. They foolishly, as it turned out, decided to make a stop-over in Java, and were caught there and put in separate concentration camps. Before leaving Singapore, they had seen to the sending of all our household goods, which never arrived, since the ship was torpedoed, put enough money in a "nest egg" to carry me through to adulthood if needs be, and sent a telegram to the headmistress of the school, naming her as my guardian. The telegram never arrived, however, and my uncle claimed me as his responsibility so I flew from Perth to Melbourne, where I was met by my aunt. We went by train to Orange, where they were living. Orange was a beautiful little place in the mountains of New South Wales. After a period of time we moved to Sydney. I was with my aunt and uncle for three and a half years.

The war ended, and my parents received a letter from me via the Red Cross, the first they knew that I had not stayed in Perth. They had been reunited following their time in the concentration camps, and after waiting several months were finally able to get away on an Australian troopship and come to Australia. Eventually my parents and I went back to Perth and I was put in the same school that I started in.

Below is a list of memories Claire Koster has of the war years when she was in Australia.

- Some private schools in Perth were evacuated to the countryside, where it was felt they would be safer in case of an invasion.

- We were given "dogtags" to wear. (identification tags to be worn around the neck.)
- Our classrooms were very primitive – wooden buildings on stilts with canvas sliding windows and tin roofs. The latter were painted brown and green for camouflage.
- Air-raid shelters were built, consisting of a trench covered with wire fencing and tree branches, with just a small open area in the back for us to crawl into.
- We had "browned-out" windows which were covered. No outdoor lights were permitted.
- At school we were each given a glass jar with our weekly ration of butter. These were kept out on the porches in wire boxes hanging from the ceiling, covered with a wet "gunnysack" to keep them cool.
- We had victory gardens and grew vegetables.
- In those years knitting was something everybody did, from small children on, and I remember knitting "socks for soldiers."

A Canadian Experience
Childhood during the War: The Hon. Rev. Walter F. McLean P.C., LL.D., D.D

Life in Canada during the war included preparing for invasions that did not occur, keeping the civilian population safe and on alert, contributing to the war effort, supporting the military through hospitality, and learning to live with uncertainties. The following is an account of life in Canada in those days, through the story of Walter McLean, as presented by his wife, Barbara McLean.

Walter grew up in Victoria, B.C. Canada and holds a B.A. from the University of British Columbia and a Master of Divinity from Knox College, University of Toronto. He undertook graduate work in theology at the University of Edinburgh. He holds two honorary doctorates from Canadian universities and has received numerous other awards and recognitions.

After leaving the University of Edinburgh, Walter served as President of the National Federation of University Students in Canada and then spent five years with his wife Barbara in Nigeria.

Barbara was a secondary school teacher and he served as a university chaplain and as the West African Director of CUSO, the equivalent of the U.S. Peace Corps.

On his return to Canada, he was co-founder of the Canadian Centennial's "Miles for Millions Walks" in 1967, and then designed and marketed the province-wide Centennial celebration in Manitoba in 1970.

During his distinguished career, Walter served as Minister of Knox Presbyterian Church, Waterloo Ontario, and as a City Councilor. In 1979, he was elected to the Canadian Parliament, remaining as an MP until 1993. Appointed to the Canadian cabinet, he was Secretary of State for Canada, Minister Responsible for the Status of Women, and Minister of Immigration. For eight years he was the Parliamentary delegate of Canada's Delegation to the United Nations in New York.

After leaving Parliament, Walter founded a consulting company as a vehicle to combine his extensive life experiences and public service in offering visionary and insightful advice to both public and private sector clients. He has over 40 years' experience as a Public Sector leader who has worked at the local, provincial, national and international level.

He is married to Barbara, who was appointed the first woman to the position of Deputy Clerk of the Presbyterian Church in Canada. She now works with Walter in their consulting company. They have four married sons and ten grandchildren.

Wartime Memories Of A Canadian Schoolboy
The Hon. Rev. Walter McLean

I grew up in the Fairfield area of Victoria, B.C., which overlooked the Strait of Juan de Fuca and the eighteen miles of water to Port Angeles in the state of Washington. All ships coming from Asia or Latin America had to come through this Strait enroute to the ports of Vancouver, B.C. or Seattle, Washington. The area had been the site of military installations during the First World War. Soldiers dug trenches in 1915 along the Dallas Road a half block from the house which was to be our family's home, beginning in 1938. The sense of military importance of the Victoria and Esquimalt harbours was always a large part of conversation among our neighbours. This area had been of strategic military importance as early as the 1870's and the Crimean War, when the British military considered the threat of another war with Russia. At that time a pair of four-ton guns were installed at Finlayson Point at the south end of Victoria.

At the outbreak of World War II in 1939, three acres of Clover Point four blocks away from my home were expropriated for military purposes. In 1947, the dismantling of these remnants of war began. I cannot drive by today or walk around Clover Point without thinking of the military camp that was there and the search-light battery and gun emplacements that were active.

My early memories as a boy of six in 1942 were of blackouts across the city with Air Raid Patrol (ARP) wardens walking up and down the streets to see if any lights could be seen. My wife Barbara, who grew up in Vancouver, has the same memories. My parents, Rev. Lewis and Frances, assembled wooden frames covered with black tar paper, which were inserted behind the curtains. My father, as chaplain of the Canadian Scottish regiment, was forty pounds under the qualifying weight for overseas service with his regiment. This was a bitter disappointment, since a number of his classmates and contemporaries in the ministry of the Presbyterian Church in Canada were off with the Canadian army, navy or air force. My father was, however, appointed Command Chaplain for the army and air force for Vancouver Island. The navy, of course, has always had its Pacific base in Victoria in the Esquimalt harbor. My wife's uncle was based at Esquimalt during the war. Our home at 63 Linden Avenue was a welcoming centre for visiting chaplains and others who were stationed in the Forces.

A number of the troops wished to be married, and the front living room of our home was very often the site of weddings, with my mother hurriedly rounding up another neighbor to be the witness of the ceremony. She was the mother of two energetic little boys, who were impressed by uniforms coming and going. The war years meant that my father received a Class A gas certificate to purchase petrol. This was to permit him to travel to the military barracks on the wild West Coast of the Island. Sunday mornings he would leave at 6 a.m., conduct two services for the military at these remote bases and return to St. Andrew's Church in downtown Victoria, where he ministered for thirty-four years, beginning in 1938. There he conducted 11 a.m. and 7 p.m. services, followed by a young peoples' social event, at which often hundreds of young service personnel would sing songs and enjoy refreshments. Next door to St. Andrew's church was a large rooming house called Robert House. Many of the troops who had overnight passes from their bases would stay there.

The impact of the war was felt by young and old alike. The imposition of the War Measures Act by the federal government meant sweeping powers over arrest, detention, censorship and control over shipping and other forms of transportation. Rationing also became part of everyday life. In 1941, rationing included meat, butter, sugar, tea, coffee, gasoline and other commodities. I can recall how little sugar our family rationing coupons would provide. Our rationing books covered not only these items but a number of others, including rubber products, which were very scarce.

After a Japanese submarine surfaced off the west coast of Vancouver Island and shelled the Estevan lighthouse south of the village of Tofino, concerns were raised about possible Japanese air-raids. As a student in Grade 1 at Sir James Douglas school, I was outfitted with a gas mask and we had regular drills in the school when we put on our masks and huddled on the grassy bits between the rocks in the school yard. Our part was to gather any fat from family cooking and to bring cans of fat to school. This fat was used in the production of munitions, we were told.

After the attack on Pearl Harbor on December 7, 1941, homeland defense had become an important priority for coastal Canadian communities. Our neighbours on Linden Avenue were part of the Auxiliary Firefighters, and our garage mechanic mobilized auxiliary firefighting equipment. As school children, we were taken to see this equipment. At our home, we had pails filled with sand and others filled with water, in case of an emergency. Garden hoses were kept ready for use in each home. Since all street lights were off at night, I recall my father was provided with caps for the car headlights which allowed only a narrow slit of light to warn approaching cars. Many adults felt it was safer to stay at home. All motorboats and sailboats were kept ready in case of the need for a Dunkirk-style exodus. Regular air-raid drills were held not only in the schools but also across the community.

By the summer of 1942, the threat of a Japanese invasion of Vancouver Island was being taken seriously. Many families felt it prudent to send women and children to the safety of the interior of the province of B.C., or even to Ontario. My earliest travel memory is of a 1942 train trip when my mother took my three-year-old brother and me to stay with her sister in Ontario for the summer. The trip was taken partly due to safety concerns and partly because of her homesickness for her family. We traveled for five nights and four days in a "settler" train car. The seating areas were converted into upper and lower berths, and we took our own food. My mother took her turn with other families in preparing our food, and since there was no refrigeration, it was necessary to leave the train at stops to find milk. I recall being frightened when she left the train, and was happy when she always returned.

The cost of the war in human terms was brought to my attention dramatically when our neighbour's son was reported missing, the news sent by telegram, and then confirmed dead. I had seen him in his uniform before he went overseas. By May of 1945, I was a student at Glenlyon Preparatory School in the Oak Bay area of Victoria. I vividly recall that after a soccer game, we were trotting beside the Headmaster back to the school to shower, when a runner was dispatched to the school to meet us. He shouted the triumphant cry, "The War in Europe is over!" It was very emotional, since the parents of a number of the students were overseas and actively involved in the war effort. A few months later, during our summer holiday on the east coast of Vancouver Island at Parksville, the sirens sounded, cars honked and word spread of the Japanese surrender.

It was nourishment, after all
and it was all, some days,
tulip bulbs, potato greens,
to satisfy our hungers. For young
and old it was the same. Not
a proper diet, but we survived
on what would bloom later
over graves of the lost
over fields of plenty.

As the war continued, food supplies became scarce everywhere, but especially in those places that were ravaged by bombings or intrusions by the military, which amounted to long-term occupation. The invading armies managed to find the best of whatever food was available, but even they suffered malnutrition where the local food supply was limited. The children of Holland were among those who experienced severe hunger, as the people there struggled to maintain a barely adequate diet. One source of nutrition for them were the plenteous tulip bulbs, and were resorted to as food when other sources were unavailable. To eat what was a source of beauty added to the value of these potential blooms.[26]

Perhaps the worst of the hunger conditions, however, took place in Russia during the siege of Leningrad – a true famine. Provisions there had been burned, the water supply cut off, and the increased numbers in search of food added to the burdens there when retreating Russian soldiers headed for the center of the city to escape the German army. Not only were the numbers of hungry increasing, but to add to the tragic conditions, winter was a brutal season of cold, made worse by the long siege. It was difficult to heat and light homes during the long nights. Corpses lay beside the Neva River, where the people attempted to get enough water every day for their needs. To buy food required ration

---

[26] Sjoerdje Daumme, *Children of the Storm,* 50.

books and standing in long lines at the shops for the very few items available which might sustain the families. Even crumbs became a delicacy in such circumstances.[27]

crusts of bread . . .
that almost sweet smell of yeast and flour
baked with the crisp outer skin flaking off
and memories of plates piled
with meat and potatoes and beets
the flavor of borscht with sour cream
layered over the brothy bowl . ..
food is mostly memory with even the crumbs
delicious forever

Even though Japan was a perpetrator in the war, initiating attacks against other countries, the people there suffered from hunger just as did those on the other side of the conflict. Food was a scarce commodity, with rice becoming a luxury instead of a regular staple in meals. Potatoes might be found, or at least potato greens, but there was a constant shortage of meat and fish, as well as tea, butter and sugar. No one dared waste food, no matter how small the amount remaining.[28]

rice is worth more than gold
potatoes are like hymns to the earth
the children root through the leaves
seeking rotted sustenance
a fish swimming dark waters
is like silver that pays with its body
what is the cost to the future
starved for hope

The people of Cyprus felt the pangs of hunger as well, in a land under British rule at the time. Children experienced keenly the inadequate food

---

[27] Lyudmila Anopova, *Through the Eyes of Innocents,* 35-36.
[28] Hiro Soeda, *Children of the Storm,* 70.

supplies for growing bodies. Fortunately there were fruits and vegetables growing in the rich soil, which kept them from starving, as slight as these amounts were. Those near the ample Klareos River, however, could add crabs and eels to their diet.[29]

> *so slim our chances for food*
> *so slim our bodies, a feature unsought*
> *when we were hungry, to be fat*
> *was a goal,*
> *the end of war tasting*
> *so sweet to our tongues*

By 1942, the children in Finland were feeling the ravages of hunger. In fact, all those remaining in their homes suffered from lack of food. The drive to survive meant to make something lifesustaining from what was available for nourishment. The lack of adequate nutrition took its toll on the health of those suffering because of the war. Non-combatants, in many ways, suffered as greatly as the members of the military. Not only did they die in larger numbers, but they were being involuntarily forced to accept the shortages of food and other necessities. It was a time that called for courage and ingenuity. The Russian troops drove the Finnish civilian population away from their homes and farms, and once the troops had been pushed out near the end of the war, their homes resembled a scene of devastation. The people found a wasteland when they returned home.[30]

> *making do:*
> *means relying on strengths*
> *we discovered in the discards*
> *of a former world means we*
> *could make do with not much*
> *we could eat scraps we used to*
> *throw out for the dogs*

---

[29] Andres Joanides, *Children of the Storm*, 105.
[30] Sirkka-Lüsa Rantanen, *Children of the Storm*, 37.

we could find the yeast
to leaven our lives now
means we could learn
what we need to know now
without letting go

In the Netherlands East Indies (Indonesia), lack of good nutrition brought severe results in its wake, most of which occurred in the Japanese-run concentration camps set up for non-combatants. Families were separated, usually the men and older boys from the women and girls. As the war continued, there were increasing deaths because of malnutrition, infections and diseases such as malaria and pneumonia. Acute hunger took its heaviest toll on the children, who had little to distract them and little energy for games. The brutality of the prison guards prevented the most basic of neighborliness among the prisoners. The Red Cross packages of food and medical supplies were retained by prison officials and did not reach those in the camps who were in great need. At war's end some who made it to temporary stations before being sent home to Holland died before they could embark on the ships home, or else while en route. Yet there was, even so, a spirit of endurance that had carried the survivors through the ordeals.[31]

these were not summer camps for kids
no arts and crafts or swim lessons no
letters and gifts from home or visits
by parents but always there were visits
from Death on a regular basis and there
was profound homesickness for former
lives nearly forgotten by now
when friends depart not back to home
but to the earth

---

[31] Beatrix Hilbers-Schoen, *Children of the Storm*, 72. Information is also included from books by Clara Olink Kelly, *The Flamboya Tree: Memoirs of a Mother's Wartime Courage,* and Helen Colijn, *Song of Survival: Women Interned.* The latter account has been made into a documentary by the same title, and into a movie, *Paradise Road,* starring Glen Close.

AWAY FROM THE BATTLEFRONT

there is a place
where war exists
it is here but not here
there is death somewhere else
who has heard the whistle
when the bombs come
but then they don't come
where is this war that does not exist

Even though many children never experienced war directly, they too were affected. For some it was by the absence of the terrors of war, removed from sounds of gunfire and bombs, or air-raids, or the presence of occupying soldiers, or witnessing brutality toward the civilian population. Yet unaware of battles, those children were touched by a universal effect of violence and bloodshed, loss and grief. No one living then was spared some kind of experienced pain which rippled through the world in ways never to be totally removed from human history and memory. Adults spoke of distant battles and the numbers of wounded. They saw passing trains headed for the dangers far off. They heard the sound of marching bands and watched returning heroes, limping or missing limbs. No one was exempt from the costs of battle.

Not to hear gunshots nor seek shelter
during air-raids, not to wonder who it is
who knocks on your door in the middle
of night, not to know the neighbor
who receives notice of her son's death
in a battle far from here, not to recognize
the martial music as uniformed youth
parade in news reels, offers a certain
respite from realities of the day, yet
the reckoning will come as surprise in what
will be the next war, once this one
is over.

Some families, even in the midst of war, were spared much of the suffering that others went through. It was a neutral experience for them. Children in Egypt, for example, did not face the rigors of hunger and fear. Even in Japan, the war did not directly affect every part of that country. One child did have a personal moment when he saw the face of an American pilot flying low over the rice fields where he was.[32]

> *when you can't see what there is to fear*
> *when you can't hear or speak to the power*
> *behind the planes behind the bombs*
> *the distance between what is perceived*
> *and what is real seems beyond the credible*
> *and there is instead perhaps some movie*
> *played out where the screen is just out of view*
> *until you see the face and then you know*
> *what you had not imagined*
> *that what you see is in a way yourself*
> *unrecognized*

Children in the United States experienced the war differently from those in Europe and Asia who were living in the midst of battles and related hardships. Most of them, other than children in Hawaii during the December 7 attack, were distanced from such terrors as bombings and destruction of homes and public buildings. Emotional damage, however, could last for years afterward. One who grew up during the war years remember that time with regret: "I think WWII destroyed my family. I remember fear being a dominant emotion during those four years. My mother barely could cope, and I was her oldest. Well ...that which does not kill us makes us stronger."[33]

---

[32] Mamoru Mitsui, *Children of the Storm*, 115.
[33] Patricia Holladay, high school classmate of the author.

family systems under fire from fear or change
can fall apart even though far from real
bombs and bullets, even without air-raid
sirens and shelters of earth
it is when the birds refuse to sing
and the bright wings of hope flutter
into stillness

yet . . .

somehow into the deep and dim rooms
Endurance teaches her lessons in spite
of failures of faith and loss of grounding
the strength of fear is cousin to
the fear of strength yet we stand firm
without understanding how

For Americans, the loss of their President through death just before the war's end was a heavy blow to their morale. President Roosevelt died April 12, 1945, and the nation wept. Children who were too young to grasp the meaning of a war witnessed the sorrow of a nation along with the sorrow of those who lost loved ones in the war, and the grief of others became their grief. They absorbed the energies surrounding such pain and recalled it years later, in spite of their inability to understand those events at the time. They could feel the spaces that were left.

we turn away for a moment
only to find emptiness where
we were when someone beloved
was with us where some leader
no longer holds power but is
gone from us forever and we think
if only we had not looked away
that space would have been full
and life would be the same would
be the same would be the same
as it always was

Mark Turner shared with his grandson the story of his life in Texas during the war. He wrote: "The memories I have of WWII are those of a young boy about your age. I was five years old when America went to war in 1941. I was nine years old when it ended in 1945. I will tell you about some of my memories."

I remember worrying very much about my Dad having to go to war. He received his draft notice and was fully qualified to serve in the army and my Mom and I were really afraid that he would have to go overseas and fight the Germans. Fortunately though, Dad was a commercial bus driver for Kerrville Bus Company in Austin, and he was needed to transport soldiers to and from training bases all over, so he didn't have to go into the army. Even though he was away from home a lot during the war doing his job, that was OK because we knew he was still in America.

I remember filling boxes (usually cigar boxes) with things to send to the soldiers overseas. This usually included toothbrushes, toothpaste, washrags, soap, razors, and whatever else I could stuff in the box.

I remember getting a stamp book at school and buying stamps to put into it for five to ten cents each and when it was full it could be turned in for a government savings bond. The money went to help the war effort. Of course Mom and Dad gave me the money to buy the stamps, but I remember how proud I was when I would completely fill the book with stamps.

I remember that we saved everything that could possibly be used in the war effort and put them in a huge wire enclosure in front of the capitol building in Austin. This included old tires, cans, tin foil (which was kinda like aluminum foil) and anything else made of rubber or metal. I don't remember saving plastic. (It probably wasn't invented yet.)

I remember that sometimes we had practice blackouts where every building and house had to turn off their lights and cars and trucks had to cover their headlights with tape, leaving just a little slit for light to drive by. The reason for this was to prepare for a possible air-raid by German bombers. I remember when I had the measles, and during a blackout one night, planes from Bergstrom Air Force Base close to where I lived were dropping parachute flares over the city to simulate a bomber attack. I saw a flare land in a field pretty close to the house, and I really wanted to go out and get the parachute, but Mom wouldn't let me because I was too sick. Some other kid got the parachute. Drat!

I really remember rationing very well. Just about everything was rationed to insure that our soldiers got first choice of everything they needed to fight the war. This meant that we often had to do without a lot of things. To buy something, you had to have a ration coupon for it, which you took to the store, but even then you might not get it because the store might not have it in stock. Even candy and bubblegum was rationed. I never ate much candy or chewed bubble gum, but if I could get some, I would take it to school and sell it for more than I paid for it. Bubble gum cost a penny and I could easily sell it for a nickel!

These are a few of the things I remember about WWII the most.

My high school classmate, Nancy Carkin Lantz, shares these reminiscences about the war years. She lived in Lakewood, Washington, near the city of Tacoma. Fort Lewis, where I lived, one of the largest army posts in the country, was about ten miles away. Students at Fort Lewis attended Clover Park Sr. High School with residents of the Lakewood area. We were in the class of 1951.

Home Front Memories

Many things have come to mind about WWII experiences. McChord Field and Fort Lewis were close to Lakewood. A neighbor was a cook at North Fort Lewis, and I was invited to join their family several times to eat with them at the Mess Hall.

My grandmother, who lived next door to our family, decided to have a small house built on the property up the hill from her big house. While the house was being built, she lived with one of my aunts and rented out the big house. A couple of small families rented her house, but one renter was a general with a house boy. I later found out he was the Commanding General and overseer of the building of the airbase, McChord Field.

During the war, we had gasoline rationing and had displayed on our windshield a sticker which noted our allotment of gas. I think we had a "C" sticker, and my uncle, who later moved into the big house, had a "B," as he was a chemist at the Pennsylvania Salt Company in Tacoma and needed more gas for driving to work each day. That was not the only rationing we had, though.

Each family member had a ration book in their name. When my mother applied for hers and didn't have a birth certificate (the small city hall in Montana where her records were had burned), she had to produce witnesses (of course) at the birth. These ration books contained coupons for meat, shoes, sugar, tires, and gasoline. Each one had a value and when the purchase was for less than that value, tokens were given as change. Red tokens were for meat. (Years later, the piano tuner found one in my daughter's player piano and didn't know what it was, but I did.) Of course you had to have the money, too. Gasoline costs today remind me of the rationing.

Mother made blackout curtains to cover the living room windows. We had a great view of the lake and Mount Rainier, when she was "out." Daddy was one of the air-raid wardens in the area, just to make sure no one built a fire that could do fire damage and to be on call should anyone need first-aid. He attended classes and we three girls were in awe of the whole thing. Daddy worked for the Northern Pacific Railway Company in Tacoma. (Mother's father had been the station agent at the nearby Village of DuPont before he died.) Daddy knew when the troop trains would be leaving, especially in the evenings, and we went to the Depot to bid the men good-bye.

Travel was limited, in addition to the limiting of gasoline. One night we needed to drive over to Clover Park High School where one of my sisters was to play in the orchestra for a program. We were driving the back way with dim lights instead of going over the lake's bridge and were stopped by a soldier wanting to know our business. Kind of spooky!! Also, we were not able to make our annual trip to the ocean for a vacation for several years, as most of the West Coast was under alert/watch for possible Japanese infiltrators. Years later, we went to the ocean and saw where the Army had built bunkers. (There had been some landings in Alaska and who knows where else. Recently I saw a movie of a California landing. How true, I'm not sure.) We saved all kinds of things for the scrap drives: Rubber, paper, metal, and I think fat or bacon grease. In grade school we were given identification disks to wear on a chain, and we had air-raid drills and were instructed to go to the basement of the school and/or hide under our desks until the all-clear was sounded. Savings stamps were sold once a week and when you had accumulated enough, a book full, they were traded for bonds. During this time President Roosevelt began the March of Dimes, with dime folders distributed to those interested. They were to be filled and were to be used for fighting polio. I thought this was important because during first grade, we had had an epidemic, and the school picnic was canceled. One of our classmates was stricken with the disease and we never heard from her again.

One more thing: Tacoma had been the home for many Japanese-Americans. After the war began, they were trucked or sent by rail to camps in California. Our family had been buying vegetables from a Japanese family in South Tacoma when this occurred. Many who had Japanese cherry trees chopped them down in protest against the bombing of Pearl Harbor. It was not a pleasant time for those who had sympathy for the innocent people.

When VJ (Victory over Japan) Day arrived, it was a beautiful and warm day and I was wading in the lake while trying to catch minnows, when I heard my uncle's bell ringing. Instantly knowing the war was over gave me, and all who heard the ringing, great joy.

Patricia Halvorsen Holladay answered her grandson's questions about her memories of World War II. Below is an excerpt from that account.

You cannot imagine growing up during a war that could intrude into your home town at any moment. My concerns were watching for enemy places on Sundays with my fourth-grade teacher ...on a plane-spotting tower no less ...hearing rumors of Japanese subs in Puget Sound...and subs shelling Astoria, just across the Columbia River in Oregon. Gas and food rations. Blackout curtains. Air-raid practices. And the sound all night of planes taking off and landing at McChord Field, just north of Ft. Lewis. Toward the end of the war, seeing German prisoners of war working on the road leading to Ft. Lewis. Watching battalions of soldiers march down to the dock, past our house, then turn around and march back to the North Fort. They always rested beside the road that ran next to our house, partly on our property. I am pulling together a model of courage, and of hope, and World War II posters reminding us that "we could do it." As the oldest, and my mother the youngest in her family, I found myself being *her* model. I feel a patriotism that may have been lacking in younger people until 9/11, (2001). Comic books were very popular: Superman, SuperWoman, Cat Woman. All super human. All able to rise above any problem.

With The Mennonites

The Mennonite tradition has a historic principle of peacemaking. In times of war the majority of those eligible for military service choose some alternate way to serve their country. Here are a few stories from the peacemakers in our culture, as they remember the war years.

Random memories of Robert O. Zehr, Mennonite pastor, describe his experiences and their effect upon his growing up years.

I Remember

I was an avid reader [of the *Philadelphia Record*] and from a young age of nine followed the beginnings of the war in Europe and then finally the Pacific. Dad was in his 30's at the time and subject to the draft. We made a move as a family in 1941 to a farm near Bridgeville, Delaware, which is still in the family. I remember the practice runs of bombers and fighter planes over our farm. At first it was exciting, but as the horror of the war dragged on it became a nightmare. As the stories of death camps began to filter through to us, I could almost scream, wishing the never-ending sounds of war above our home would go away.

(Many years later, after visiting the Holocaust Museum in Jerusalem: As we exited the museum on a dark and rainy day, the old feeling of dread that the sound of bombers and fighter planes elicited in me in the early 1940's came back.)

I remember food stamps, ration stamps, shoe stamps, gas rationing, tire rationing, blackouts, as well as the black paint on the upper half of car headlights. I remember cutting asparagus in the morning. Our high school at Bridgeville dismissed morning classes so that the crop of asparagus in the southern Delaware region could be harvested. We joined a large group of German prisoners who cut asparagus in neighboring fields. At the end of the war an official from Washington, DC came and presented our school with a flag and a certificate. We had helped win the war by cutting asparagus, he said.

At the close of the war, I had to register for the Selective Service System. I was drafted and assigned to an alternative service, which I served in Middletown, Connecticut.

Rosella Wiens Regier shares the memories she has of conditions her family lived under in Kansas.

Hard Times on the Farm

I was a child of Mennonite parents who believed in peace. Our congregation spoke of it often. Most of the young men of draft age went into Civilian Public Service in WWII and into I-W service in conflicts since. During WWI, the men went to military plants or camps to serve in menial tasks and were often persecuted.

I was a child during WWII and accompanied my parents on very infrequent shopping trips to McPherson, Kansas, from our little town of Inman. There at Anthony's Store my parents spoke German to each other as they contemplated a purchase. They were asked to speak only English, since Germany was our enemy. I remember being so embarrassed; now I have pride in my parents' courage.

Those were hard times on the farm. My four brothers were all of draft age and were ALL drafted. With poor equipment and few resources, it was a very tough time for my parents to make ends meet and also do without the labor of the boys. What I remember about those years was our poverty, but mostly the farewells at the train depots when our young men went to "camp" (CPS). Girlfriends stayed at the back of the crowds to say farewell last. Parents wept. Children were bewildered. Our brothers and sons were leaving for places unheard of before. Would we ever see them again? When they stepped on the train platform, the family or crowd sang, "God be with you till we meet again." There was hardly a dry eye. Places like Ypsalanti, Michigan; Terry, Missouri; Boulder, Colorado; Hagerstown, Maryland; Belton, Missouri – they rolled off my tongue eventually as my brothers wrote letters and told stories later. Projects called for mental health workers, barbers in mental hospitals, sugar beet harvest, watch towers and fire fighting in forests.

One young man in my church chose to enter the military. My pastor, with a heavy heart, brought him his "excommunication from the church" papers on the eve of his departure. My parents were very, very sad about that and saw it as a most unloving way for the church to uphold morality.

The writer of this piece, Ann Towell, grew up in a Mennonite family on a farm in Indiana. Her memories are of loss and her subsequent hatred for war.

Experiences of Sadness and Small Joys

I was born in 1930. On the Sunday that the war in the Pacific began, I was on my stomach in the living room reading the funny papers. My dad said, "This is it," and from that time on it was War. My dad's brother, who was 35, joined the Marines; my cousin, whose parents were Mennonite, was drafted. He served in the South Pacific as a driver for a Medic. My mother's three brothers were drafted. One, a doctor, served in the Army, and one, the youngest of eight children, served in the South Pacific. The thing I remember was that when my grandmother died while they were gone, she "visited" my uncle on her way out of this life. The third uncle was in the Air Force, and was stationed on the west coast as a repairman on airplanes. My dad was always one year older than those being drafted, so never served. The movies always had vivid pictures of the fighting. To this day I won't view war pictures.

We had rationing. ABC cards for gasoline. Sugar and meat were rationed too. It's just as difficult for me to relate this as it was to live through. I have a distaste for war that is overwhelming. My brother-in-law was one who went to the Korean War and didn't return. I always felt guilty that he and the boys I went to school with were required to go to war and I wasn't. I grew up with all of them; girls didn't go. Joe was killed and two weeks later, Sonny, one of the orneriest boys who ever drew breath was killed after only six weeks of training. Then at least five kids my age or older were killed. I don't plow through this pain very often, and won't do it again except to explain my aversion to war of any sort.

Now back to WWII. At the beginning of the war in Germany, my dad told me of the death camps. It wasn't broadly talked about. But he always knew the worst and darkest things. We lived in the farmlands of Indiana, and I don't remember the blackouts, except one when I sat outdoors on the porch steps to see if there was any light to be seen. I have always wondered, because that night I saw a group of lights that traveled in a line. There was no noise of motors. All was silence. I have always wondered what it was I saw. There was also the sighting of the most outstanding lights I have ever seen from the *aurora borealis* – blood-red they were and lasted for more than one or two nights.

I was old enough by then to do farm work. One summer I drove nine tractors, doing the work of men who weren't there. I learned to shuck oats and wheat, mow hay, and cultivate corn. I never want to live through another time like that.

War is hell!

A retired doctor in Philadelphia, Pennsylvania, Len Byler, recalls several wartime memories of his childhood growing up in an Amish and Mennonite community. Those in the peace churches who were eligible for military service, as noted previously, for the most part became conscientious objectors and served in non-combatant roles.

Brief Thoughts of Wartime Childhood

In WWII, I was in early grade school. The only war injury for this Amish-Menno kid was being called "CONSCIE" at the public school. Felt ashamed. And then, ashamed of my shame; lacking in strong personal peace conviction in first through fourth grades.

Closest the war with Germany came to the Amish farm community in Big Valley was the nightly blackout warnings, with regular peals of the town fire siren as reminder. Not really many lights at our place anyhow. But the kerosene lantern wicks would be lowered further if they were burning, and we'd speak in hushed tones for awhile – in German! (*Pennsylvanii Deitch*)

Barry King once performed mission work in Africa, flying planes and serving in other capacities. He describes an incident at a dinner table in Kenya during the mid-1970's.

At the Dinner Table

My passenger [on my mission plane] was a Dr. Hans Grüber from Germany, a missions executive visiting a bush hospital at Lokori, in northwestern Kenya's Turkana district, with a view to the possibility of increasing their already-generous funding of that hospital. Our host at Lokori was a Dutch nurse, Ms. Jaani Vanderklis, whose work was supported by Dr. Grüber's mission. So at that time they were both, so to speak, playing on the same team, with shared objectives about humanitarian work in Africa. But over dinner, the conversation turned to the war, which at that time was only 30 years in the past.

I asked Jaani about her experiences during the war, and she told about how she and her family used to huddle in the basement of their house as the bombs dropped on their town from *Luftwaffe* airplanes overhead. She asked Dr. Grüber about his own experience. He was silent for a moment, and then said, "I was a navigator for the *Luftwaffe*."

Homefront

The experience of African-American children and families during the war not only included the common ones as shared in these stories, but they also had the pressure of living in segregated communities in the South and in other parts of the country as well. Lewis A. Brandon, III, grew up in Asheville, NC. He graduated from NCA&T University in Greensboro, after which he served in the military during the Vietnam War era. After his military service, he taught science first in high school in Greensboro and then at NCA&T, where he also conducted scientific research. For a time he worked with the Foundation for Community Development in Durham, NC. Now retired, he is the Coordinator of the Grass Roots History Project at the Beloved Community Center in Greensboro. His memories of the war follow.

I remember seeing military convoys and troop trains coming through the Asheville [NC] area. My father (Lewis A. Brandon, II) and a neighbor (Harold Burton) were Pullman porters, and they were exempt from the draft, the only two young men in our neighborhood who didn't go into the service. My cousin, Thomas Waters, served overseas with the US Navy. I recall being aware that all the younger men from our neighborhood had disappeared, gone into the service. My father, a great uncle, Albert Jordan, also known as "Wank", the neighbor who was a porter with my father, and a local barber, Mr. Jacobs, these four, were left of the friends and family. All the servicemen I knew of were in segregated units, because during that time the military was not integrated.

My father was gone a lot with the trains transporting troops. We lived not far from the railroad crossing, so whenever we knew he would be coming through, we'd go wave to him as the train went past. At least we got a chance to see him that way while he was working.

Our neighbor Wilbur Rone didn't go into the service either, but instead went to work at the Oak Ridge Laboratories in Tennessee, not far from Asheville. And because we were so close to Oak Ridge, I remember blackouts where we lived. I guessed it was for security reasons.

I remember the day my Aunt Parthenia got the telegram saying that her husband, Herbert Porter, who served with the 761st Tank Division, had been injured and her coming off the front porch as she ran to tell a neighbor. The 761st was the first African-American tank battalion to see combat in the Second World War, and was recognized for its bravery in combat. Those men were in four major battles in Europe and sustained many injuries and losses. My uncle was sent to the Army hospital in Battle Creek, Michigan to recover, permanently paralyzed from the waist down. He finally came home, but was in constant and terrible pain, and about ten years later committed suicide rather than continue to live with the pain.

Some of the German prisoners of war were sent to the Asheville area. The government had taken control of several facilities there. I know that the German officers were housed at the Grove Park Inn, a resort hotel, and the Grove Arcade was also taken over by the military until maybe the '70's. It has since been redeveloped into shops and restaurants. The

Grove Park Inn is in an area, Beaverdam, settled by many Jews because they could not live in upscale Biltmore Forest or buy residential property there. But the German officers were billeted at the resort facilities in a community predominantly Jewish.

My Uncle Wank brought the news to us about the death of President Roosevelt. People gathered on our front porch to listen to the funeral on the radio. Some were crying and talking about what a wonderful man he was. They said that he saved the country by bringing it out of the Depression. He started the CCC (Civilian Conservation Corps) that put a lot of people back to work. They thought Roosevelt was kind of like a Moses, and they were really saddened when he died.

I also remember when the war ended. Uncle Wank was a bell captain at Battery Park Hotel and he came home announcing the end of the war in Europe. We all piled into his car and went to Pack Square where crowds were shouting and celebrating. My cousin, Bobby Seymour, who was a teenager, rode the running board of the car as we joined the crowd in a joyous day for us all.

Mary Lu Cawood Sanders grew up in Kentucky and now lives in Greensboro, NC. She remembers what it was like during the war years for her and her family.

My parents raised rabbits so we could have meat, and I learned how to kill and skin a rabbit. I was in the fourth grade and on the Monday following the attack on Pearl Harbor, we gathered in Miss Kelly's room at Kenwick Elementary, in Lexington, Kentucky to hear President Roosevelt's "we have nothing to fear but fear itself" speech. All the students learned what to do when the air-raid sirens went off. We had blackouts, too. I had no elastic in my underwear and one day walking to school, my underwear fell off.

Later, on hearing the news that the war was over:
I heard the paper boy shouting, "Extra! Extra! The war is over!" In a few months Daddy was able to get some new tires! Daddy was the Director of the Lexington/Fayette County, KY Health Department and as such, was in a "frozen" job position [meaning he could not leave it] until

after the war was over. When he got those new tires, we moved to Middlesboro, KY. That's where I met Don, my husband, and the rest is 52 years of history.

What does it mean when your enemy does not hate you?
How do you say thank you to those you prepared to hate?
What is stronger than resentment?
When you are hungry the odds begin to change.
When you are frightened you see life in a different measure.
When you have known only fear and distrust of those
who would do wrong, those you were taught to despise,
how can you be grateful when nothing is what
you believed to be true? How do you say thank you
and accept the kindness of strangers?
When did your perceptions turn, manifested in what you
did not know before?

As the war entered its last months, adjustments were required in determining who would continue to be thought of as enemy and who would remain an ally. In Germany, lingering battles and enmities continued near the final days of the war. Boys had been recruited to serve in those times, still in their teens, some as young as 12. Their determination to continue fighting rested on an unrealistic idealism to save their country from defeat. After D-Day and the subsequent battles brought American tanks into towns where residents surrendered, children experienced a different kind of military personnel, who came into the towns peacefully. It was also a time when children encountered black soldiers for the first time. The troops handed out candy and fruit in an attempt to show that they would be friendly to the townspeople. Those who lived in areas where the British and Russian soldiers came through often had mixed experiences, but many of the soldiers did make efforts to show kindness to the battle-weary residents. In addition, American charities sent food to Europe to feed the hungry, in the form of CARE packages.[34] It may have been a surprise for many to discover that

---

[34] Werner, *Through the Eyes of Innocents*, 191.

when war comes to an end, former enemies seem as familiar as one's neighbors, especially for those children who had never met anyone from a different land other than the enemy who brought devastation from a distance, seldom face to face.

> *those overdrawn caricatures of enemies*
> *or spoken descriptions in exaggeration*
> *define them until we see face to face*
> *the mirror of our face*
> *the common human connection*
> *and we are surprised*
> *to have been so deceived*

The realization comes slowly that because of our common humanity, we need not live in a world where we must separate nation from nation, community from community except by free choice. One form of that awareness came to many as they experienced the presence of prisoners of war. Some labored on farms, some lived with families. They were French, Russian, German, Italian, depending on which side had captured them. These were the fortunate ones, able to avoid prisoner-of-war camps and instead serve in the countryside, where a labor force was necessary to replace the men away in the military. Relationships developed and friendships were formed, or at least the recognition that these "enemies" were more alike than different in their natures. The regret is that it takes a brutal war to come to such realization.[35]

> *the problem with war is that it separates human*
> *categories so that we learn early to hate*
> *and see only the difference that creates enemies*
> *war solves that problem when we find ourselves –*
> *all of us – to be human and nothing more*

During the last days of war in Germany, news broke about Hitler's suicide in his bunker along with others who had stayed with him out of

---

[35] Erwin Perrot, *Children of the Storm,* 121.

loyalty. Some of the German people, especially the youth, felt that they had been betrayed by Hitler and his staff, and any further battles would bring only senseless bloodshed. What would be the purpose if even their leader had abandoned them through choosing death over defeat? They would continue to question the whole purpose behind the German war effort and the aim of domination over other nations.[36]

It doesn't come immediately, the awareness of truth;
its elusive nature is elsewhere, avoids our beliefs.

Truth cannot lie, does not betray, yet we pursue
only what we are told to seek, only the false façade.

Without its presence, meaning has no meaning,
and there is betrayal in the very wind that sweeps

across this scarred earth, when those we trust
deny their promises, and we are left with dust.

In spite of the losses and devastation that took place in Germany during the war, there was appreciation afterward for the care received from Allied soldiers. These kindnesses made a difference and provided the vision for a future without wars, the hope of a lasting peace. Elsewhere in the war-torn areas, that same vision and hope came because of the absolute horror the people had lived through. The worst was the bombing of Hiroshima and Nagasaki in Japan with a new and heretofore undreamed of weapon, with its atom-smashing consequences. The children of the detention camps in Asia, the concentration camps of Europe, the siege and starvation in Russia, and all such terrors were enough to demand a future which never again would see such destruction. From the perspective and aftermath of many more wars since that time, the vision of such a peace remains as always in a time that has not yet come. The children of this war, however, maintained the hope and the dream.

---

[36] Dieter Borkowski, *Through the Eyes of Innocents,* 135.

The scars will cover pain absorbed
by time, yet nothing removes recall
of sirens and shelters and birthing
that lend unwonted clarity to a child
who believes all of life is the way
that it happens for them and nothing
can alter or make it better.
Yet hope, that unremarkable feature
of all life when unfettered slips through
with balm for fear and something new
to enter this inaccessible portal of terror.
It is the remarkable birth that is focused
on the future. It is the promise we hold.

A major obstacle facing some families was the rearrangement of borders, so that returning home was not possible, when "home" as they knew it had disappeared in the mists of war. Children in Finland understood this, when areas had been ceded to Russia. The challenge for them was to find work to help their families, and many labored in the fields of farmers who still had their land.

Boundaries shift and home is somewhere else
as though we are simply markers on a game board
without attachment to the land. We were starved
for home, whatever that means when war displaces
everything familiar and in the return not to where
we were but return nevertheless. We must
do what we can and live with hope.

Children have a gift for recovery and resilience, in spite of what they have endured. Whether it was hunger or fear or separation, these children were able to hold on and bounce back. It was evident in the aftermath of this war, as children everywhere saw themselves in a new light, scarred emotionally no doubt, but as capable of meeting the future, whatever that might be.

we were empty in soul and body
defeated and unaware and without
a way out yet we were young
and we were elastic

In the United States, the experience for some was the reverse of what others dealt with in war zones. Life became exciting and adrenalin was pumped into the spirit of the people. For them, this had been a popular war, complete with villains and rescuers. And there were those as well who realized that the war could bring a fortune to those whose interests were self-serving. As a child, I once overheard adults speak of wishing that the war would go on a long time because they could make a lot of money from it. I didn't know why that would be true, or what kind of work they were in, but the conversation disturbed me. I could not imagine how anyone would want war to continue. Yet to my surprise, there were indeed those who were profiting from a situation that promoted killing others. It might be years before I would be able to give such immorality a name, but I knew even then that it was wrong.

when we look at war and destruction
from a distant vantage point
so far from realities of death
when the bands and the cheers
and the movies boost our patriotism
there are scenes we don't want
in the make-believe war

When the Japanese homefront received news of the war's end, there was great sadness instead of rejoicing. Not only had they suffered the eternally damaging horror of two atomic bombs wreaking a destruction unknown in history's previous wars, but their dreams of great world power had been dashed. Some went to the palace of Emperor Hirohito to apologize for their failures to achieve success in the war. In the United States there were parades and cheering crowds. In Japan, there was silence in the streets. They had been unable to honor their emperor with victory. They mourned their dishonor.[37]

> *Strangely dispersed, unequally accepted*
> *by the blameless for the sins of their leaders*
> *the blanket of guilt slips over us all*
> *who could never do enough to make*
> *victory rise up from ashes,*
> *never be adequate to the commands*
> *of those in charge who must be heedless*
> *to suffering brought on by them,*
> *and we who acquiesce will partake*
> *of what we did not choose to make.*

The damages affected everyone finally, not simply those in war zones, or those who were barely surviving even during the best of times for others. Rich and poor, humble and influential, the war had cast its broad shadow over the world. Those who lived in Hungary, for example, of well-to-do circumstances felt the effects. Some who owned fine horse breeds were forced to move elsewhere, some to England and others to South Africa, after first stopping off in Austria and Bavaria until the war came too close for them there. The children were able later to understand that this experience provided a wider range of understanding as they shifted their lives from protected and comfortable conditions to those of adapting to new and uncertain environments along the paths of their escapes. Their horses became their instructors.[38]

> *Even the worst of times*
> *confounds despair, dares fate to make indelible*
> *what destroys, what betrays expectations,*
> *contains a glimmer of promise.*
> *Yet fear that rides the saddle of night,*
> *the drone of enemy terror, the terrible cry*

---

[37] Masachika Onodera, *Children of the Storm,* 150.
[38] Countess Hanna Jankovich-Besan, *Children of the Storm,* 150.

of uncomprehending horses
must defeat hope for the moment,
delay blessings that come with change
waiting beyond the stables in new pastures.

An understanding of the effects of war on children involves more than one criterion for gauging how the power of early experiences will carry over into adulthood.

The trauma of war appears to affect children differently, depending on the level of violence they have been exposed to and their capacity to cope with it. The effects tend to vary also with their age, gender, and temperament; their family and social support, and the political ideology and/or religious faith that provides the context of their lives. Some war experiences in childhood tend to have a lasting impact: Exposure to heavy bombing and combat; prolonged separation from the family; internment in refugee or detention camps; the loss of loved ones through acts of violence; and lack of proper schooling.[39]

These memories can mark a child indelibly, carried into adult life by way of fears and anxieties that become part of other experiences which ordinarily would not evoke such reactions. Memories are triggered by some event that becomes embedded in one's later life. War is never forgotten.

memories tattooed with horror –
they hold permanent patterns
forever within our spirit
and we can only overwrite
the worst of them
it is easier to deny anger
or fear that invades dreams
is it possible to pretend
to be normal after all that
oh cry oh weep oh grieve
what you cannot claim as yours

---

[39] Werner, *Through the Eyes of Innocents,* 211.

A seven-year-old girl living in Honolulu at the time of the attack on Pearl Harbor retained memories "of fear and horror as a war began without warning just a few miles from our family's home." Later, living in Oregon, she and her family returned for visits. "Now, we take our children and grandchildren back to Hawaii to see the *Arizona*, still visible just beneath the surface of the water. There is little else to remind us of that Sunday morning when bombs fell from the sky and children awakened to learn that their world was no longer secure."[40]

> *we cannot live forever in that time*
> *life refuses to indulge our memories*
> *yet we know and we remember*
> *so that grandchildren will be witnesses*
> *to our stories*

Memories for children in the European war theater were strongly laced with fear and terror. The remembered siren sounds, the air-raid shelters with crying babies and frightened adults, the overpowering dank smell of the earth surrounding them, remains for a lifetime. The conviction that such events must never again take place is also a result of these experiences. Never again a war. Yet our histories since that time show that these determinations have been disappointed many times over, as each war in turn makes way for the next one.

> *Reminders of earth stenched by human use survive*
> *in nostrils depriving memory of moist soil*
> *rich with smells of life blooming to fullness.*
> *Forever lingers the shrill song of the sirens of death.*
> *We learn that never is what happens despite our hope*
> *in every moment. Yet we cannot forgive the stink of war*
> *on earth, our good earth, earth of home. Never again,*
> *we swear, never again, never must the raven of death*
> *dare cover itself in false purity.*

---

[40] Alice Belt Faust, *The Day Our World Changed,* 80, 83.

Never again must children remember
forever what dirt smells like underground
what hunger tastes like what fear feels like
never should they ever know this for the rest
of life and afterward in the dark earth.

This account by Eileen D. Morman, who grew up in England, describes her
life during the war. She later married an American and now lives in Greensboro,
NC. An excerpt from this appears in a previous section of this book.

Reflections on World War II

The war started when I was thirteen years old and ended when I was nineteen, so the "teen years" were not like young people today enjoy. Everything at night was closed. The movies ended the last show before 9:00 p.m. because all the buses stopped at 9:00 so that people could get home or wherever they were staying because of air-raids; in addition it was because we had a complete blackout after dark.

One scary time was when I was in high school. The rule was that if the air-raid siren went off we had to run home, because there was not an air-raid shelter at school. So one day the siren sounded and we were running home when I heard the sound of a German fighter plane. During a class we had been taught about different aircraft and also about gases. So I glanced up and there it was, coming right at us, machine guns firing. I lay flat as possible between the sidewalk and the road. The plane passed over us. There were three of us going in the same direction, and we were lucky that day because we were all right. Later on we heard that a plane had been shot down, maybe the one firing on us. The school decided to put an air-raid shelter under the school yard after that incident.

My home was in Plymouth, England, which is near the coast. There were many bombings; gas works and electric plants were all bombed during one long air-raid. We were without all those utilities for quite a while. The water wagon came twice a day, and we were allowed a bucket of water each time. We still had a wood-coal big oven and stove, so my mother was able to cook meals on that. Some of our neighbours brought their dinners to be cooked. We had good fresh vegetables, thanks to my dad's expert gardening. Our rations consisted of two ounces of sugar, two ounces of margarine, and one egg a week, and a lot of other food was rationed. Sausages were not rationed, so about once a month the butcher shop would make some. We were allowed one pound to a customer; it meant standing in line for sometimes two or three hours, but it was worth the wait.

Young women also were "called up" to serve in the military at age 18, so I went into the Women's Royal Navy Service (W.R.N.S.). Our nickname was "WRENS." It was a time in my life that was a great experience, meeting others from all walks of life and making friends with such a great group.

Somehow through it all we kept our sense of humour and our strong belief in God. That, I believe, is what helped to make our wills strong.

War is a terrible thing, no matter who is involved. Lives cannot be replaced; the destruction is devastating, and in the end, what is the real meaning of it all? We grow old still "seeing" every now and then and remembering people we knew who were lost forever. May God rest their souls in peace. Perhaps one day people will accept that we are all part of the whole of God's creation and embrace each other so that peace will at last come on this earth.

The American military at that time was for the most part segregated, as noted earlier. The following account is shared by William Howard about his older brother's experience as a black soldier during a critical battle in France, when Howard was a teenager too young to serve in the military. He now lives in Greensboro, NC where before retirement he was Editor of the newspaper The Carolina Peacemaker.

As my brother George Howard boarded the small craft that was about to land on Normandy Beach during World War II, many of his black comrades expressed their fear of death. As gunfire and bombs were seen and heard on the beach where they were about to disembark, one voice shouted, "Lord, help us! Why must we fight and die for people who hate us both here and in our country?" My brother became very fearful and angry. When the landing boat hit the shore, he ran only a short distance and decided to hit the sand, and remained in the same position for many long hours. He told me of the many bullets that flew over him and of the bombs that exploded not far from him. He watched many of his black brothers get shot and either killed or wounded. The battle lasted most of the night. Somehow he evaded the bullets and the bombs. His greatest prayer was answered.

Later in his life, my brother George Howard graduated from New York University and eventually received both his Masters's and Doctoral degrees from NYU via the GI Bill. He lived to fight racism and injustice for the rest of his life. Often he spoke to me about doing the same with my life. I have not let him down. He fought a war against the Germans as well as against racism. Together we learned that racial wars never end, especially since we grew up in the ghettos of Harlem and Brooklyn, New York City.

CLOSING REFLECTIONS

Courage comes in many forms. One form of courage is for children of war to move forward without hatred, leaving behind a better world than they entered as children.[41]

Children are repositories of the world's memories. In times of war, they absorb through their senses the tastes, smells, sounds, sights and feel of fear, of terror, of violence, of the deepest pangs of hunger. These memories sink deep into the very cells of their small bodies, to affect them years later in a variety of expressions. The stories contained in this collection reflect the memories of those who spent their childhood in the turbulent times of what is commonly known as World War II. For many, the experience was one which defined loss for them: Of family members, of pets, of homes, or simply of a way of life which had seemed safe and predictable.

Children in the United States were not exposed directly to the power and destruction of warfare, but they too went through a time of dislocation and disorientation from the familiar. They may have discovered new strengths and ways of coping with the drastic changes to their lives because of rationing or absence of the male family members who had represented stability and authority. Their mothers, aunts, cousins often went to work to aid the war effort or to bring in additional income. Some developed independence because of a new status as "latchkey children." Some learned to adjust to having only one parent at home with them. Others experienced the constant worry that those they loved would not return from the war, or else would be terribly wounded. The newsreels, the movies, the newspapers, the radio programs all reflected the times, and often fed their fears.

William Tuttle, in his study of American children during the war, noted that "nothing was more unsettling than the father's departure for

---

[41] W. E. Samuel, *The War of Our Childhood: Memories of World War II,* from the Epilogue, 348.

military service. In other families, the wartime absence of an older brother was equally upsetting. The safety of uncles, cousins, and neighborhood fathers and brothers also concerned boys and girls. These were anxious and painful years for the homefront children.[42] He points out that "about 183,000 homefront children lost their fathers."[43] Their fears were all too often realized. Other fears may not have materialized, but for some children, these were of deep concern, nevertheless: "Throughout the United States following Pearl Harbor, children feared that enemy bombs might rain down on them too. Their anxieties deepened as they participated in air-raid drills and blackouts."[44]

American children also reflected the ideologies of their nation, the patriotism which abounded, the sense of pride in their country. The alternatives would have been bordering on treason, in their perspectives, and were not voiced to anyone despite possible doubts about the meaning of war. Tuttle comments:

"...there could not have been a more impressionable time for children to be exposed to the heavy doses of the patriotism and democratic ideology that prevailed on the homefront. This was a war between good and evil; there were no shades of grey, no nuances, especially for America's school-age children. Ranging in age from five or six to puberty, these girls and boys learned well the lesson of their country's righteousness before all nations, imbibing it in their schools, churches, and theaters. Indeed, although feelings of invincibility and moral certainty were two qualities widely shared by the school-age children, another was a sense of personal self-worth, motivated by participation in the war effort."[45]

Children from other parts of the world, however, remembered not only these experiences, but also the afflictions of war where they were living. As the experiences in this collection indicate, they are memories laced indelibly into the minds of those who lived through those years of

---

[42] William Tuttle, *Daddy's Gone to War: The Second World War in the Lives of America's Children*, 30.

[43] Tuttle, *Daddy's Gone to War*, 44.

[44] Tuttle, *Daddy's Gone to War*, 5.

[45] Tuttle, *Daddy's Gone to War*, 115, 112.

war. They knew the destruction of their homelands, the losses too many to list, the fears and anger with residual emotional effects on their psyches. Children, we say, must be spared the adult evils that abound in life. Yet we continue to layer evil on evil, as the years since that world war have been laden with other wars, other battles, other destruction. And we noted earlier that more than 95% of those injured or killed are the non-combatants in today's deadly conflicts. Children are among them. The wars go on.

In our own time, a UNICEF report explains that "an estimated 20 million children have been forced to flee their homes because of conflict and human rights violations.... more than two million children have died as a direct result of armed conflict over the last decade. More than three times that number ... have been permanently disabled or seriously injured. More than one million have been orphaned or separated from their families."[46] The report also lists the hardships children undergo, situations that reflect many of the same ones cited by those in this collection:

Children in armed conflict also routinely experience emotionally and psychologically painful events such as the violent death of a parent or close relative; separation from family; witnessing loved ones being killed or tortured; displacement from home and community; exposure to combat, shelling and other life-threatening situations; acts of abuse such as being abducted, arrested, held in detention, raped, tortured; disruption of school routines and community life; destitution and an uncertain future. Some even participate in violent acts. Children of all ages are also strongly affected by the stress levels and situation of their adult caregivers.[47]

We realize that war, whether a matter of history or a time we currently live in, has its familiar evils that now are magnified because of more "sophisticated" weapons and thus an impersonal involvement by the military in many cases. The inhabitants of our planet have seen the

---

[46] UNICEF:"Child protection from violence, exploitation and abuse,"
http://www.unicef.org/protection/index_armedconflict.html?q=printme.
[47] UNICEF report

results of warfare, have received the warnings to civilization, have begun to gather in organizations and international peacemaking efforts to stop this unsuccessful way of resolving the disputes among nations. The act of war must be forever removed from the options of this world's inhabitants. There is no justification for either offensive or defensive warfare any longer. Former war correspondent Chris Hedges, in his "Introduction" to the book *Iraq: A War*, makes this assessment: "War is, finally, always about betrayal. It is about the betrayal of the young by the old, idealists by cynics and finally soldiers by politicians. Those who pay the price, those who are maimed forever by war are crumpled up and thrown away."

We must speak for the children of our world. In another age, the prophet Jeremiah spoke to an incident not unlike this modern one, a reference quoted later in the Gospel of Matthew:

A voice was heard in Ramah, wailing and loud lamentation, Rachel weeping for her children; she refused to be consoled, because they are no more. (Matthew 2:18)

All the Rachels of the world weep for the children. They weep for themselves as well. They weep for those they have loved, who are no more: The old women, the old men, the sisters and brothers, the cousins, the aunts and uncles who hovered over their families with gifts and love. Rachel weeps and there is no solace. These are the children of God, the God who weeps uncontrollably, who is like a woman piecing together scraps of fabric. Yet there is that in God the One who is the Gatherer, the Gathering God. The God who gathers up the torn and tattered pieces from our lives, worn and discarded, useful no more for they have no purpose, who gathers something valuable from all the bits and pieces. She creates a new thing: A tapestry of many colors, worked into one piece, whole and useful.

This is the God who gathers all the broken and torn lives, the sorrows and grief of destruction, of lost children, dead children and lost hopes.

See, I am going to bring them from the land of the north and gather them from the farthest parts of the earth, among them the blind and the lame, those

with child and those in labor together, a great company, they shall return here.
(Jeremiah 31:8)

This God speaks to Rachel: *See, I bring all the lost from the wars and violence wherever they are. I am a Gathering God, and all who are lost will come home to me forever. They are with me. My arms hold them. They are comforted. I am a Gathering God. All those who have lost their homes, their loved ones, their children, their parents – all who have lost their cities and communities – see, I gather them to me so that they may live with hope in my promises. I am a Gathering God who makes all things new – who brings surprises to those who have lost their hope, to Rachel who has lost her children. I, their God, am here with them, with you, with all my people.*

Sources and Resources

Ahearn, Lorraine. "Pebbles from a 'Kindertransport.'" *The Man Who Became Santa Claus and Other Winter Tales.* Greensboro, NC: Cold Type Press. 2010.

Anderson, C. LeRoy and Joanne R., Yunosuke Ohkura, Eds. *Not Longer Silent: World-Wide Memories of the Children of World War II.* Missoula, Montana: Pictorial Histories Publishing Co., Inc. 1995.

Bowles, John, Ed. *The Day Our World Changed: December 7, 1941: Punahou 52 RemembersPearl Harbor.* North Liberty, IA: Ice Cube Press. 2004.

Chittister, Joan, OSB. From an interview at Chautauqua, July 2008.

Colijn, Helen. *Song of Survival: Women Interned.* Ashland, OR: White Cloud Press. 1995.

Frank, Anne. *Diary of a Young Girl.* Mumbai, India: Wilco Publishing House, Inc. 2006 edition.[one of several different publishing houses which have published this]

Goossen, Rachel Waltner. *Women Against the Good War: Conscientious Objection and Gender On the American Homefront, 1941-1947.* Chapel Hill: UNC Press. 1997.

Harris, Mark Jonathan and Deborah Oppenheimer. *Into the Arms of Stranger: Stories of the Kindertransport.* NY: MJF Books. 2000.

Hedges, Chris. "Introduction." *Iraq: A War.* Olive Branch Press/Interlink. 2007.

Higa, Tomiko. Dorothy Britton, trans. *The Girl with the White Flag.* NY: Dell Publishing (Little Yearling Book). 1991.

Hoopes, Roy. *Americans Remember the Home Front: An Oral Narrative of the World War II Years in America.* NY: Berkley Books. 1977, 2002.

Jones, Wilbur D., Jr. & Carroll Robbins Jones. *Hawaii Goes to War: The Aftermath of Pearl Harbor.* Shippensburg, PA: White Mane Books. 2001.

Kelly, Clara Olink. *The Flamboya Tree: Memories of a Mother's Wartime Courage.* NY: Random House Trade Paperbacks. 2002.

Keuning-Tichelaar, An and Lynn Kaplanian-Buller. *Passing on the Comfort: The War, the Quilts, and the Women Who Made a Difference.* Intercourse, PA: Goodbooks

Kindertransport and KTA History. http://kindertransport.org/history07_KTAoverview.htm.

Lee Li-Young. "After the Pyre," from *Behind My Eyes.* NY: WW Norton & Co. 2008.

Perkins, Charles. *Children of the Storm: Childhood Memories of World War II.* Osceolo,WI: Wordwright Books (previously); MBI Publishing Co. 1998.

Rosenblatt, Roger. *Children of War.* NY: Anchor Books. (Anchor Press/Doubleday). 1984.

Samuel, Wolfgang W.E. *German Boy: A Child in War.* Jackson,MS: University Press of Mississippi (originally in a hardcover version). 2000.

The War of Our Childhood: Memories of World War II. Jackson, MS: University Press Of Mississippi. 2002.

Smollar, David. "Letters home in 1945 reflect joy, concern after atomic blast," special to the *Los Angeles Times,* reprinted in the Greensboro, NC *News & Record.* No date.

Tuttle, William M., Jr. *Daddy's Gone to War: The Second World War in the Lives of America's Children.* NY: Oxford University Press. 1993.

UNICEF Report: "Child protection from violence, exploitation and abuse." http://www.unicef.org/protection/index_armedconflict.html?q=printm e. 2006.

Werner, Emmy E. *Through the Eyes of Innocents: Children Witness World War II.* Boulder, CO: Westview Press. 2000.

DISCUSSION GUIDE

This Guide can be used when a group reads the book together, or simply for the individual reader to reflect upon after reading the book. It is presented according to the sections included in the book. These questions and statements can be used to develop other conversations and discussions. If you read this as a group, you may want to address each section as you go through the book.

The Beginning

If you were living during the time of the Second World War, do you remember first learning about the Japanese attack on Pearl Harbor? How did you hear about it? Who was with you?

How did you react to the news?

If you were born after that war, has anyone described what it was like to live in that time? Was it a family member, friend, teacher, someone else who told you their story?

If you did not live in the United States then, what was it like where you were? What was happening before the US became directly involved?

Have you read any histories about the beginning of the war, and events that led up to that moment when the United States entered it? How did you react to the stories in this book, with your background knowledge of the war?

In the poem about the Japanese woman whose sons were in both the Japanese and American armies, what would you say to comfort her?

Relocating the Children

Perhaps you, as a child, had to move to another location. Did it have to do with a war somewhere, or a family move or change in your personal circumstances ? What feelings did you have about making such a change? What were the results?

Do you find these accounts of children who were forced to leave their homes, either to be in a safer place or because of other necessities related to the war, something that you could relate to in some way? Share that story with others.

What is it like to be taken from what are familiar surroundings and sent somewhere completely unknown to you? How might you try to make the necessary changes in your environment?

The Dark of War

This section is difficult to read. How do these stories of children and young people in the midst of warfare compare to your own life? Suppose you were the parent of one of these children. How would you relate to that child's experience?

The German boy, Ernst, tells of his experience helping his father care for the wounded following an allied attack. How did such an account affect you if you were on the other side of that conflict? Do you see any universal emotions in his story? How did his own attitude toward the war change during those days? Consider how yours might do the same, in similar conditions.

Are there situations today related to warfare that might be similar to these stories? Perhaps you have been in such a time yourself. If you are willing to do so, share how that was for you.

One element that stands out in these experiences is that of fear. Think about the effects of fear upon a child, and how fear affected you as you grew up.   Do you continue to have that same emotion when remembering such a time for you?

Some readers, like a few of the stories in this section, may also have been heavily affected by the war, but not directly involved in it. Can you recall what it was like to be in such a situation?

There have been numerous wars since World War II, and many of the same elements can be found in them as well. How might you relate to what was happening as told by these contributors, as it took place in your own life during a later conflict?

Hunger

Have you ever been hungry? Were you able to satisfy that hunger easily? Consider what it might be like to be hungry over an extended period of time, with only limited sources of nourishment to sustain you. How might your outlook on life be affected by that hunger? Put yourself in the shoes of one of these contributors, imagining yourself to be in that story. What insight might you receive from doing so?

Picture a dinner plate with nothing but a few bites of a grain food or vegetable or rice, with perhaps a taste of fish or meat. How would you adapt to such a diet on an extended basis? What might be the effect on your view of food and eating today, after such a time during the war?

Away from the Battlefront

Even those who were not living in the daily struggles and dangers of war were affected by such a time. If you were a child during the war yet not living in a war zone, what were some of the ways the war affected your life? Think of family members who served in the military, or the items that were rationed, both food and other items. There were many movies about the war, that may have glorified those events in order to stir patriotism. These were viewed by those on all sides of the war, along with other propaganda as a part of daily fare. How did you react to such as that?

Several of the stories in this section are written for grandchildren, to explain what it was like to live in a time of world-wide warfare. Write something for the young person in your life, detailing your experiences. How are the wars that have followed that time of war different or similar with times then? Do you feel as deeply affected by current wars as those who contributed stories to this book?

For those who served in the military who were of a different racial background than the main body of troops, how were their lives different? If you belong to one of those groups, how does reading their accounts affect your perspective of that war?

Looking Back

Some of the children who were living in conquered areas and living under occupation by the victors of the war, the Americans, the British, and the Russians in particular, tell of their surprised reactions to meeting those who formerly were the enemy, face to face. How did they react, and what would have been your reaction?

Some contributors speak of their resilience following the war, in beginning new lives after such destruction. What were some of their perspectives at that time? If you were living in one of the occupied countries then, how did you relate to the changes brought on by such circumstances?

What were some of the social changes that took place in this country as a result of the war? Were you or any of your family affected by those changes directly?

Closing Reflections

The comments in this section include some statistics about the effects of warfare on children. Could you add to those out of your own experience?

Chris Hedges notes that war is about betrayal: Of the young by the old, the idealists by cynics, and soldiers by politicians. Would you agree with that statement? How might you differ with his assessment?

The final passages of the book refer to biblical sources about Rachel and her children. The point is to show that the lasting solution is not war and tragedy and loss, but the bringing of life out of death by God's healing power. What part does your own faith play in your perspective about war, and if you are not a person of faith, what ideas sustain you in times such as war? What arguments or conclusions can you make about the whole nature of war, not only as it affects the life of children, but the effects of war upon all people as well as the environment?

What can you do to work for peace in your lifetime?

About the Author

Jean Rodenbough is a retired Presbyterian minister living in Greensboro, NC. A poet and writer who has published books on fiction, poetry and pastoral care, she is active with the North Carolina Council of Churches and other organizations working for peace and justice. She is a Benedictine Oblate with the community in Erie, PA. Her husband Charles is a historian and writer. Their four children and families live in the Greensboro area. She has served as a chaplain for hospice and with hospitals. She received her MA in English from UNC Greensboro, her M.Div. degree from Duke Divinity School and her D.Min. degree from Columbia Theological Seminary. Her interests also include chip carving and playing the recorder.

ALL THINGS THAT MATTER PRESS ™

FOR MORE INFORMATION ON TITLES AVAILABLE FROM
ALL THINGS THAT MATTER PRESS, GO TO
http://allthingsthatmatterpress.com
or contact us at
allthingsthatmatterpress@gmail.com

Made in the USA
Charleston, SC
06 January 2011